KENT AIRFIELDS
in the
Battle of Britain

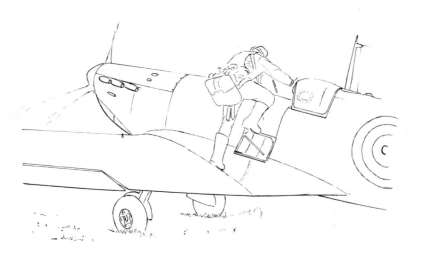

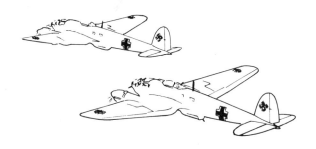

KENT AIRFIELDS
in the
Battle of Britain

THE KENT AVIATION
HISTORICAL RESEARCH SOCIETY

MERESBOROUGH BOOKS

Published by Meresborough Books, 7 Station Road, Rainham, Gillingham, Kent.
ME8 7RS

Meresborough Books specialize in the publication of books on Kent local history. Twenty-four books are currently in print with more scheduled for publication Summer and Autumn 1982. In addition Meresborough Books publish a monthly journal on all aspects of Kent local history, 'Bygone Kent'. Full details from your local bookshop or direct from Meresborough Books.

HAWKINGE 1912–1961
An in depth history of the former RAF Station
By Roy S. Humphries

Published as a uniform edition with this book, also at £5.95. Available from your local bookshop or direct from Meresborough Books at £6.40 post free.

KENT'S OWN
The story of 500 Squadron, Royal Auxiliary Air Force
By Robin J. Brooks

To be published as a uniform edition with this book in July 1982, also at £5.95.

First published 1981
Reprinted (with some revision) 1982

© Copyright 1981 KAHRS

ISBN 0905270 36 3

Printed and bound by Mackays of Chatham Ltd.

CONTENTS

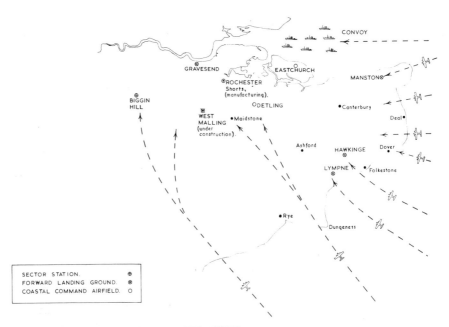

THE FIRST PHASE: GERMAN PLAN FOR TOTAL VICTORY.

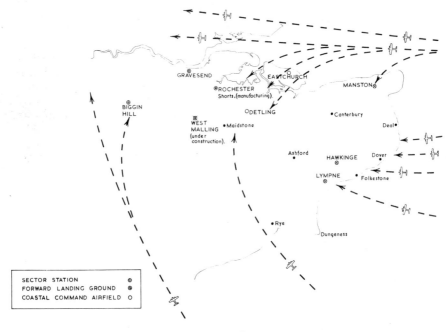

THE SECOND PHASE: ATTACKS MOVE FURTHER INLAND.

INTRODUCTION

This book, as the title suggests, is about the Battle of Britain airfields of Kent. It is not a history of the entire battle nor, indeed, of the war itself. Its main point of interest is 1940, and that period from mid-August until late-September, when the battle centred upon those airfields that the Germans believed available to No. 11 Group Fighter Command.

For the Royal Air Force, the Battle of Britain started in July 1940. That was when the Luftwaffe, using recently captured French airfields, began their attacks upon merchant convoys using the Straights of Dover. It was a short and desperate phase, and one in which the Germans hoped to demonstrate the true might of their air forces.

A second phase of the battle started very soon after. The Germans, aware that radar was in use, attempted to destroy a number of the south coast radar stations. They came within an ace of success but, unaware of the true import of this invention, they abandoned this plan for the more tangible rewards of an all out attack upon RAF airfields in South East England.

For the Luftwaffe, the Battle of Britain started on August 13th, 1940, and the day officially designated as ALDER TAG (Eagle Day). It was the day on which the enemy concentrated itself entirely upon the RAF's front line airfields. The day started with an early morning raid upon Eastchurch, and the near devastation of this aerodrome. The afternoon witnessed a massive raid upon Detling, and an attempted raid on Rochester. For the airfields of Kent, this was also the day that the battle began in earnest.

It is this last phase which is the central point of interest for this book. In those dark, desperate days, the RAF was constantly subjected to attack. Fighter Command on the ground, and in the air, could never rest secure. In one continuing process the airfields of Kent were continually put out of action. Biggin Hill, Eastchurch and Manston were constantly battered, but just as frequently they were repaired and again ready for use.

This is the story of those airfields.

PHILIP MACDOUGALL
Publications Officer, Kent Aviation Historial Research Society

ACKNOWLEDGEMENTS

Members of the Kent Aviation Historical Research Society would like to thank the following who have assisted in the writing of this book. In all cases, names appear under the subject heading for which they gave most help.

BIGGIN HILL
Wing Commander I.H. Cosby DFC, RAF Retired, Mrs D.E. Finnie, Mr E.D. Williams, Mr M.D. Mumford, Mr D.B. Goodchild, Mr and Mrs D. Gee, Mr S.R. Roberts, Mr J.S. Nelson, and Mr J.R. McDonald, M.O.D., Air Historical Branch, RAF. Putnam Publishing Co. for use of 'RAF Biggin Hill' by Graham Wallace and also Jane's Publishing Company for use of 'The Battle of Britain — The Hardest Day, 18th August 1940' by Alfred Price.

DETLING
Ex Flight Sergeant John Thompson, Squadron Leader S.W. Jarvis (retd), Pat and Jack Hoskins, Mrs Jean Johnson, Mr Bill Yates, Mr Jim Dunlop, Mrs Doris Owen and Mr Douglas Pain. Special thanks are reserved for Ann Griffiths of Offham whose untiring help in contacting former members of 500 Squadron was of considerable help.

EASTCHURCH
Mr J.E. Rutland, Mr F.J.R. Gillen and Mr P.J. Small.

GRAVESEND
Christopher R. Elliott for the use of various documents.

MANSTON
Mr A.T. Gifford, Mrs Vera Green, Mr Henry Green, Mr Ken Wallis and Squadron Leader W.L. Grout.

ROCHESTER
Mr John Chinery and Mr C. Gilks.

AIRFIELD DEFENCES
Mr Henry Wills, Mr David R. Barnes, Mr Ron Crowdy, Mr Geoff Harvey, Mr Reg Curtis, Mr Chris Vincent, Mr Bill Smith, Mr Wally Kingsford, Mr Albert Stone, Mr Harman, Mr Frank Cruttenden, Mr A.T. Gifford and Squadron Leader W.L. Grout.

ABOUT THE KENT AVIATION
HISTORICAL RESEARCH SOCIETY

The KAHRS was formed several years ago by a number of aviation enthusiasts living in Kent. The aim of the society is to research, record and reproduce the history of aviation in Kent. Although fairly small, members have gone some way in recording the history of aviation in Kent. Apart from numerous published articles written by individual members for local magazines and papers, the society has helped and advised the media by providing background information on this aspect of the county's history. Furthermore, the society recently produced its own booklet 'Wings Over Kent' which has now sold out.

This book has been written by members of the Kent Aviation Historical Research Society and a little information about their background is given below:

ROBIN BROOKS has been an aviation historian for 10 years and is a founder member of KAHRS. He served his National Service in the RAF in the trade of Operations Clerk in Air Traffic Control. Previous articles have appeared in 'Kent Life', 'Bygone Kent', 'Journal of Kent Local History' and numerous local newspapers. His future plans include a history of 500 Squadron, Kent's Auxiliaries and further articles on local airfields. Robin has two daughters.

DAVID G. COLLYER. Co-founder and archivist of KAHRS; specialist in Kent aviation history and defences. Former member of Kent Branch 'Air Britain', published works include histories of Ramsgate, Bekesbourne and Lympne aerodromes as well as contributions on aviation and local history to local press and county magazines. Born in Deal 1937, worked 20 years as Architectural Technician, present post Assistant Purser on Sealink ferry M.V. 'Vortigern'.

PAUL GRUNDY. Drawings and cover design for the book have all been produced by Paul. For a number of years now, he has been specializing in aviation art and hopes to make this a full time occupation. An ex-member of No. 99 Folkestone Squadron Air Training Corps and Kent Gliding Club. Most of his spare time is currently spent renovating his cottage at Smarden.

ROY HUMPHREYS. A founder member and chairman of the KAHRS. In 1940, as a boy of twelve, he was a first hand witness to the battles being fought in the skies of Kent. Since 1968 he has specialized in researching Hawkinge airfield and, inspired by a tremendous sense of history, raised a memorial stone at that airfield in 1978. His book on Hawkinge is being published simultaneously with this volume. He has contributed on aviation subjects to many books and magazines.

PHILIP MACDOUGALL. Publications Officer of the KAHRS. He is a school teacher and enthusiastic local historian. Most of his researches are directed towards North Kent and he has recently had a book published on the Hoo Peninsula.

RAY MUNDAY. A founder member of the KAHRS, he is a local government officer, married with two children. He served for two years in the RAF on National Service and has been interested in aviation since a boy. Has specialised during the last ten years in Kent aviation and Gravesend airport.

LEN PILKINGTON. The only flying member of the KAHRS, Len has taken a number of the aerial shots used in the book. As regards airfields his main specialisms are Joyce Green and Horton Kirby, but flying mainly from Biggin Hill it would be hard to ignore the stirring history of that airfield.

Chapter One
KENT AND THE BATTLE OF BRITAIN

By Roy S. Humphreys

In this, the first chapter in the book, I feel obliged to set the scene for subsequent chapters which, as the title of the book implies, deals solely with Kent airfields engaged in the epic Battle of Britain, a battle, according to some historians, which has become memorable in English history.

I have resisted the temptation to mention the finer edges of political or military strategy, for quite apart from the risk of boring you, the reader, the simple explanation is the quite phenomenal wealth of documented intelligence available that seems to confuse even the academic mind. When we read of the intelligence net-work set up by both Germany and Great Britain, we begin to wonder how anything positive was achieved at all in subsequent battles, either on land, at sea or in the air.

There are, of course, books specially written about the Battle of Britain, books of distinction, in-depth analytical studies of each day's events heavily documented and, without doubt, of immense historical interest. On the other side of the coin there are others, written by combatants of both sides which convey the humour and tragedy of personal experiences, seen through the eyes of young men trained to a high degree of efficiency in their own elite force. The reasons for war and the strategic implications of battles meant little to them and they were usually unaware of the political policies. Their reasons for fighting at all were very much simplified. Most were ready to disregard political aspects, believing they were an unnecessary imposition. As a result, the combatants were just pawns in a game, who fought quite oblivious of the influences of coercion, subterfuge and sometimes treason.

It is all the more poignantly obvious therefore, that this particular battle somehow impressed upon the citizens of this nation a spirit of camaraderie, first experienced perhaps on the Dunkirk beaches, but which was especially emphasised during the individual combat of our fighter pilots in a hostile sky.

The scene is set in the year 1940, in the county of Kent, the nearest land-mass to the Continent of Europe and often regarded in travel brochures as the 'Garden of England'. In that year of 1940, it became almost overnight the 'Guardian of England', whose people were to endure the pain and suffering of countless enemy actions. Those who lived nearest to the English Channel were bombed, shelled and machine-gunned at all hours of the day and night, while those who lived further inland found themselves in the direct path of German bomber streams en route for London. In the skies above the county there was enacted a play with a cast of thousands for, as most people will agree, the Battle of Britain was fought over Kent, and around its one hundred and eighty-five mile coastline. One fact alone, that of the concentration of Luftwaffe airfields in the

This picture is a rare shot of the Le Panne Sands, just east of Dunkirk taken from HMS 'Sandown', on the first morning of the evacuation. Lines of British troops can be seen waiting for the 'little ships' to take them off to larger vessels. (Kennedy)

The oil storage tanks at Dunkirk burn furiously as HMS Sandown, heave's to just one mile from the beach. In the foreground can be seen HMS 'Oriole', a minesweeper which went aground, but which floated off at high tide. (Kennedy)

Pas de Calais area, would go some way to substantiate that Kent saw more enemy action than any other county in the British Isles.

Although the military effectiveness of the Luftwaffe operations in the European campaign brought about almost a complete collapse of civilian morale, the same military tactics when used against Great Britain, failed miserably. This was possibly due to the one particular British trait which always becomes an irritation to much of the rest of the world. I refer, of course, to that calm indifference, complete disregard or, as someone once said, 'bloody-mindedness'. Whatever the terminology, such an attitude of mind is usually emphasised when Englishmen have their backs to the wall. When faced with a desperate situation they seem able to draw on some super-human effort to survive at all costs.

The British people are a phlegmatic lot, and the people of Kent probably more so. A prime example was the occasion in 1940, when it was thought unforgivable that a quiet game of golf on the cliffs above St Margaret's Bay should be interrupted by a straffing Messerschmitt. Equally unforgivable was the occasion when an interesting game of cricket was hampered by one of the team being killed by a shell fragment. Despite being one man short however, the game continued. Surely this state of mind must be exclusively British!

I believe it was Dr Goebbels who called such absolute determination against all odds, 'pig-headedness' and stupid. Without doubt, Hitler misunderstood the importance of such an attitude. An attitude which had won for this country many victories in the past when defeat seemed all but inevitable.

Soon this corner of England was to become known as 'Hellfire Corner', all 1,445 square miles of it. One wonders if that name had anything to do with one Lieutenant Lilburn, who had been nicknamed 'Billy Hellfire' way back in 1820, when he was a customs officer of the Kent Coast Blockade. If that is just a figment of the imagination, German hostility was not. Kent was soon to bear the brunt of an aerial attack never before experienced.

The build-up began when high explosive bombs were scattered in fields between Chilham and Chartham on May 10th. A few days later more were dropped on Dover. That same week, in answer to a radio broadcast made by Anthony Eden, then Foreign Secretary, thousands of men enlisted in the Local Defence Volunteers, a civilian army that eventually became known as the Home Guard. These men were part soldier and part civilian. They were clerks, farm labourers, solicitors from towns and villages and initially without either uniform or arms of any description. Nevertheless they helped the regular Army in erecting road barricades, barricades which consisted of steam traction engines, ploughs, farm implements and carts, tree trunks, water barrels and just about everything and anything they could lay their hands to.

This operation, the first meagre line of defence, occurred before the 'Little Boats' joined larger vessels to evacuate the British Army from the beaches at Dunkirk.

There existed for hundreds of years in this county of ours a rivalry between the 'Men of Kent' and 'Kentish Men', which persisted until the Spanish Armada

Survivors of the British Expeditionary Force, rescued from the beaches of Dunkirk, head for Dover in a Yarmouth Herring Drifter, following Route Z, one of the three swept channels established for the evacuation. (Kennedy)

This German Stuka pilot is rescued from the sea and taken on board HMS 'Sandown', the very ship which shot him down by machine-gun fire a few minutes earlier, off Dover in July 1940. (Kennedy)

was given a beating in the English Channel in 1588. As history shows those 'Men of Kent' and 'Kentish Men', fought alongside each other during those sea battles. Together they kindled a great heritage, for neither Philip of Spain, Napoleon or even the Kaiser could assail these islands. When the call went out in 1940, it was largely from Kent that men of all descriptions, especially from the coastal towns, Thames-side and the Medway, who knew anything at all about boats and the sea, volunteered to man all sorts of craft from steam pinnace to paddle steamer. They sailed to France and brought back to these shores the remnants of the British Expeditionary Force. Thousands of our troops, hungry, tired and battle weary, some wounded, disembarked at Sheerness, Margate, Ramsgate, Dover and Folkestone. It was an unforgettable sight. Women of the county rallied round to provide endless gallons of tea and mounds of sandwiches. No one quite knew where the supplies were coming from, or for that matter cared. Nearly every household contributed something. It was a triumph of impromptu, voluntary effort, which gained the admiration of the nation, if not the world.

But now the British population were suddenly to become incredibly serious. There is no doubt that the situation looked very grim at the time. With the German armed forces standing along the Channel coast, looking at Kent and Sussex, our only line of defence was the 1st London Division, spread out between Sheppey and Rye. They were ill-equipped to defend the vital Dover Straits, possessing only about eleven 25 pounder field guns, hardly any anti-tank weapons to speak of, and about two dozen Bren-gun carrier vehicles. They were hardly a powerful force to be thrown against the victorious German Panzer Divisions, now poised to strike in our direction. A German invasion attempt on this island became a reality, although there has been much debate since the war as to the success. It was about this time that the War Cabinet heard these words spoken by a member of the Chief of Staff.

"Should the enemy succeed in establishing a force, with its vehicles, firmly ashore, the Army in the United Kingdom, which is very short of equipment, has not got the offensive power to drive it out ... "
The speaker went on,
"... the crux of the matter is air superiority."

Following Dunkirk, the county became a bastion. To bolster our dwindled armed forces we eventually mustered over 470,000 men into the Home Guard throughout the land, armed with 10,000 rifles of doubtful vintage, and a collection of home-made hardware which, if used, would have probably killed the user. Concrete Pill-Boxes were erected, some were disguised as sea-chalets, petrol stations, shops and even piles of logs. Sign-posts were taken down and long poles were stuck in fields to deter the expected German parachutists. Barbed-wire and sandbags seemed to be everywhere. Glass window-panes were festooned with sticky-paper to safeguard occupants against flying splinters. Roads became obstacles with concrete blocks stuck upon their surfaces to slow down the

Swingate Radar Station 1936. (Recons. Towers under construction)   (Mr Harman)

expected enemy motorised battalions. Across fields, parkland and around hills deep tank traps were dug. Iron railings, even the ornamental railings of churches and Manor house alike, were removed and taken to the foundry to be cast into guns and tanks. Street collections of aluminium saucepans and kettles found their way to the smelting-pot from which emerged the Hurricanes and Spitfires. Church bells were silenced, only to be used as an invasion warning. Local industries and factories changed over to wartime production of one kind or another. Children were evacuated to safer regions of the British Isles, and sometimes whole families were split up. Father was called-up into one of the three services, mother went into a factory. In Ramsgate alone the population dropped drastically from 34,000 to 10,000, Folkestone from 40,000 to 9,000. Both became ghost towns.

On June 18th, Churchill had said, "I expect the Battle of Britain to begin." He was right, of course. But I have often wondered if he ever envisaged the intense aerial battles, courageously fought by our fighter pilots. He later said of them, "The gratitude of every home in our island, in our Empire, and indeed throughout the world, except in the abodes of the guilty, goes out to the British airmen, who, undaunted by odds, unwearied in their constant challenge and mortal danger, are turning the tide of world war by their prowess and by their devotion. Never in the field of human conflict was so much owed by so many to so few."

The origins of Kent aerodromes is given in another chapter but it can be said here that most were constructed during World War 1. Then few held any Home

Defence squadrons to combat the German Gotha and Zeppelin raids. When the last war began, these same aerodromes were coupled to a defence system specially tailored to suit our island's needs.

In 1936, we had completely reorganised our defence structure, and Fighter Command was born with a multiple Group system with each Group responsible for its own particular area. To begin with, only two Groups were formed in the fighter role, No. 11 Group, covering the South East of England, with No. 12 Group responsible for the Midlands and the North. But, within a year, No. 13 Group was formed to take over the North and, by 1940, No. 10 Group had materialised to cover the South West areas.

Each Group incorporated what were known as Sector Stations, whose operational status would control fighter squadrons in any given area of defence. Of the seven Sector Stations within No. 11 Group only one, Biggin Hill, was in Kent. In the main, the Sector Stations had been long-established, comprising full repair maintenance, medical and Headquarter facilities. In addition, they were able to use to their own special advantage a number of forward satellite aerodromes from which squadrons could operate on a temporary basis. It was at these forward aerodromes, such as Manston, Gravesend, Lympne and Hawkinge, that the detached units could refuel and rearm and then wait on 'advanced readiness'. Because of the meagre facilities at Bekesbourne, that small airfield was never considered to be anything other than an emergency landing ground.

If the reader is familiar with the old defence concepts of the 1920's, it will be immediately apparent that the new structure of defence was a considerable improvement, providing a well organised and clearly defined operational chain of command. However, one factor, that of a modern fighter squadron using the very latest and most up-to-date aeroplanes, was not, in its self, enough to provide what could be called an 'in-depth-defence-system'. The whole essence of our defence system was an early warning of approaching enemy formations.

Up to 1938 we had relied on an established acoustic warning device manned by units of the Regular and Territorial Army, who played around with mechanical gadgetry which, to say the least about it, was little more use than a toy. Kent had more of these devices in use than probably any other county in the British Isles. But then came the most advanced early warning system ever devised — Radar.

The development of Radar-Location had advanced sufficiently by mid-1938 to enable our fighter squadrons, then mostly equipped with bi-planes, to meet opposing forces with a degree of success. At the outbreak of war, in 1939, Dover possessed a Low-Level radar station erected about July 1937, on the cliff edge overlooking the harbour. Another station, but this time a High-Level Station, was sited at Dunkirk, between Faversham and Canterbury.

These, and other radar-location stations erected round the coasts of England, provided information to Group Controllers who, in turn, passed on this information rapidly to our intercepting squadron commanders in the air.

The static radar sites, consisting of huge wood or metal towers, plotting

Pre-WWII concrete sound mirror erected in late 1920's on the Downs above the town of Hythe. It remains to this day a symbol of our early-warning devices used before the invention of radar. (R.S. Humphreys)

The latest and the most modern of the sound-mirror devices erected in the first months of the Second World War. It also remains to this day on site, just a few hundred yards west of the concrete mirror. (R.S. Humphreys)

A sound locator operated by The Royal Engineers. It was an early forerunner of radar and used in Kent during the 1930's.   (C.R.E. Library, Brompton)

rooms and electricity generating equipment, were liable to aerial attack. It was probably more luck than judgement that the Air Ministry provided a small number of mobile radar units. One such mobile emergency unit, called a G.L unit, operated near Dover ostensibly to assist the A.A. Guns, but its true potential was soon realised when it became incredibly successful in plotting German aircraft forming up over their French bases. Inevitably, this mobile unit was soon linked into the main static station, and was most probably one of the reasons why the radar network, even after suffering a bombing raid, could operate within a few hours.

Hitler's invasion plan for South East England demanded air superiority and with it, the complete destruction of Fighter Command. We now know, through studying German war documents, that Hitler's plan was rather ambitious and foolhardy. But at the time the civilian population of this country were told to expect an invasion. There seemed nothing more certain.

The German plan named 'Operation Sealion', would have parachuted battalions onto the high North Downs area behind the town of Hythe, to sweep round eastwards to capture the harbour at Folkestone. Simultaneously, the 17th Infantry Division would have beached at points between Hythe and Dymchurch. It was whilst Hitler was contemplating whether to invade, or not, that we barricaded those very beaches with scaffolding poles to which we attached mines.

Flying Officer A.V. Clowes, DFM, of No. 1 Squadron, Wittering, climbs into the cockpit of JX-B for the official photographer. Both the Hurricane and pilot were Battle of Britain veterans   (I.W.M.)

This photo shows a typical dispersal hut used by fighter squadrons in 1940. Here pilots of 46 Squadron relax at Digby between scrambles. The doll in flying gear, suspended from ceiling was a squadron mascot.

20

Pilot Officer P.W. Lefevre (fifth from right) whose father was Mayor of Canterbury, poses with pilots of 46 Squadron at North Weald   (Lefevre)

The ancient monuments known as Martello Towers, erected in Napoleon's time, were now impregnable gun positions. For miles around searchlight units and gun emplacements dotted the county like mole-hills in a paddock.

German armed forces had conquered, in just a few weeks it seemed, Poland, Norway, Denmark, Belgium, Holland and France. Now it was our turn to feel the weight of Goering's Luftwaffe, then reputed to be the strongest air force in the world. It was also our turn to show to the rest of the world what we could do.

On August 1st 1940 the Air Staff issued their policy on the role of the Royal Air Force, should the invasion occur. This gave Fighter Command the job of protecting its own organisation. Bomber Command was given the task of attacking the invasion fleets, the barges and tug-boats which were bottled up in French harbours. So desperate was our need to fling every available aircraft into the sky, that the Tiger Moths of Training Command were fitted with 20-pounder bomb racks! On occasions they flew up and down the Channel, hugging the contours of the Kent coastline completely unarmed!

Officially August 8th has been given as the day when the Battle of Britain actually started, but even this date is arbitrary, for it was not until four days later that the town of Dover felt the first real impact of massed enemy formations. However, the preliminary air attacks, the prelude to Adler Tag (Eagle Day), opened up on Channel convoys, a pattern which lasted about one month. It was in the second week of August that the Luftwaffe concentrated its efforts on the fighter airfields in the South East. Within a month most of the airfields, including the vital Sector Stations and some not under Fighter Command, had received one or more attacks. The efficiency of the command was certainly impaired,

Gillingham, Nelson Road, Bus Station. The result of a raid on August 27th 1940
(Kent Messenger)

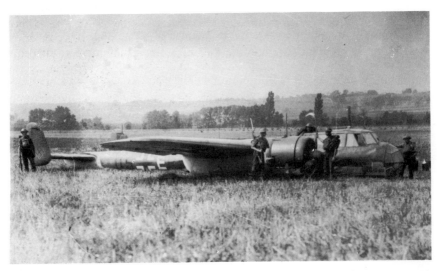

Dornier Do.17 brought down near Lenham   (Kent Messenger)

He.111 H (KC.2) shot down at Woodchurch, Nr Manston 1.8.40.

although buildings do not make an airfield. Fighter aircraft were still able to operate from suitably patched-up fields. Bomb craters were rapidly filled and earth flattened.

Once Goering diverted his attacks on London, there were few nights which went undisturbed by enemy action of one kind or another. Sirens wailed their mournful note before high explosive bombs, incendiaries, and parachute mines fell on towns and villages. A lot of the indiscriminate bombing, whole cargoes of lethal castings, were never intended for military targets. They were, instead, dropped on towns in North-West Kent to bring pain and suffering to thousands. Such was the plight of civilians in wartime. September 1940 has gone down in English history as the month when the Royal Air Force turned the scales in its favour, when it took the full weight of Goering's Luftwaffe and survived.

But at one stage in the battle we had lost, in just one fortnight, 290 fighters destroyed and 170 damaged. Replacements totalled about 260. More serious were the pilot losses, for we had lost about 300 in the month of August alone. Those are reasonably accurate figures, but during the battle period, both sides gave wildly inaccurate assessments, probably for propaganda purposes.

The tragedy concerning pilot losses over the Channel and North Sea can largely be attributed to the failure of the Air Ministry to provide an adequate, well organised air sea rescue service. Germany had provided the HE59b and HE60 Seaplanes for their sea rescue operations, but before 1940 our air sea rescue service was practically non-existent. All rescue operations at sea relied on the Royal Navy, together with the co-operation of the lifeboat service. The RAF

ME.110 crash at Key Street, Bobbing, Nr Sittingbourne   (Kent Messenger)

Dornier Do.17, Marden July 1940   (Kent Messenger)

held a small number of light rescue craft but were, in the main, only responsible for picking-up our airmen in distress after a location plot, or fix, had been established. The RAF had been in possession of a number of high speed launches (HSLs), which were eventually used from selected coastal harbours. It became a most pressing problem during the summer of 1940, to rescue our 'ditched' aircrew, and it was not until December of that year that a few Lysanders, borrowed from an Army Co-operation squadron, began searching for airmen in distress.

Nevertheless, whatever the inadequacies of a rescue service at sea, the air battles raged on unabated. Some of these air battles could last for three quarters of an hour. From the ground enemy formations looked like small black dots trailing streamers of white vapour.

Earlier in this chapter I referred to the many books already written on this historic air battle, a battle of continuous air fighting which lasted almost three months. But Sunday, September 15th, has always been regarded as one of the 'greatest days'. That particular day was described by Winston Churchill, the Prime Minister, in the House of Commons, as "the most brilliant and fruitful of any fought upon a large scale up to that date by the fighters of the Royal Air Force". Combat figures quoted for that memorable day are 60 German machines for a loss of 29.

Although the Battle of Britain is the subject of this book one cannot forget the air battles and air war which continued over Kent, almost unabated, until hostilities ceased in 1945. True, the RAF were gradually gaining air superiority from 1941 onwards, and enemy violation of the skies above England became spasmodic, but many coastal towns received aerial attacks from small enemy fighter-bomber units, usually referred to as 'tip-and-run' raids. These isolated nuisance-raids continued into 1943, and in June the following year, Hitler released his pilotless robot-bomb, the V1, better known as the 'Doodle Bug'. Launched from sites in the Pas de Calais area of France, they came over in their hundreds and, up to September 1944, over 1,388 had either fallen of their own accord or had been brought down by our fighters or A.A. guns on Kent soil. Over 1,000 had been destroyed over the Channel before reaching the coast.

To combat this 400 mph menace with a 1 ton warhead, additional mobile guns and the latest rocket launchers, firing a 3 in. projectile in batches of around one dozen at a time, were sited near coastal towns. These flying bombs caused damage and havoc, and many an unsuspecting civilian was to lose his or her life whilst shopping in the High Street, or walking in the park.

One of the worst disasters to befall the unsuspecting occurred when a flying bomb exploded on a railway line near Rainham, just as the Margate Express reached that very spot. Such was the fate of the civilian population.

Besides the bombing, be it from aircraft or robot, Kent coastal towns were also subjected to German long-range shelling. Dover and Folkestone were particularly heavily damaged and suffered many casualties as a result. Some shells carried for considerable distances, and on one occasion Maidstone felt the impact of bombardment.

The Messerschmitt Bf.109-E4 seen here at West Hythe, belonged to JG27, Luftflotte 2, and was shot down in September 1940.   (Folkestone Herald)

This photograph shows Hauptmann Artu Dau, of 111/JG51, who was shot down on 28th August 1940, by Squadron Leader P.W. Townsend of 85 Squadron.
left to right: Jack Wood (LDV), Cyril Souton (ARP), Mr Worrall, P.C. Hills   (Dover Express)

109 Forced landed at Smeeth, 23rd November 1940   (Kent Messenger)

After 'Overlord', the invasion of France, allied troops moved into the Pas de Calais area and advanced upon the German gun sites and V1 launch sites. It was then the people of Kent began to sigh with relief for the first time since Dunkirk.

This pleasurable experience was, however, short-lived for those living in North Kent, as Hitler almost immediately launched his V2 rocket on London. This was the latest and most devastating secret weapon devised by German scientists. It arrived through the stratosphere from sites in Holland to fall in and around London, without warning, and at a speed faster than sound.

For the younger generation it must be extremely difficult to appreciate that so much happened in this one small corner of England. Although forty years has elapsed since Hitler's Luftwaffe was defeated in the battles of 1940, there is still evidence of those hastily erected ground defences and airfields. For example, if we negotiate the country lanes or walk the North Downs, we will often find a concrete Pill-Box, standing sentinel-like, guarding a road or rolling farmland. They — if nothing else — stand to remind us of Hitler's threat, as the Martello Towers remind us of Napoleon's. Of the airfields in the county, so beautifully constructed for the bi-plane era, only one — Manston near Ramsgate — retains any operational allegiance to the Royal Air Force. The others have either been abandoned, taken over by civil operators, returned to farmland or had housing estates built on them.

At the risk of boring you with statistics, some idea of what Kent people endured during the war can be seen from the following figures.

111 Forced landed at Kennington May 1941 (Kent Messenger)

ME.110 at Lenham September 1940 (Kent Messenger)

War debris, Tonbridge Road, Maidstone   (Kent Messenger)

Kent had a total of 9,000 casualties, of those, 1,490 were killed and 7,516 injured. If one was to include the outer-London areas in Kent, then the total number of casualties reaches 18,065. The number of high explosive bombs falling on the county totalled 28,760, and incendiaries were 717,800. No fewer than 4,400 houses were destroyed and 190,200 dwellings were damaged.

The airfields, their names written into the annals of English history, have become part of our national heritage and, like Trafalgar, Zebrugge or Dunkirk, will never be forgotten.

Eastchurch. A pre-World War One Flying Display

('Flight' photo)

Chapter Two

THE BATTLE OF BRITAIN AIRFIELDS: THEIR ORIGIN AND EARLY HISTORY

By Philip MacDougall

The history of those airfields which participated in the Battle of Britain goes back, in part, to World War One. During those years the responsibility for defending Great Britain against aerial attack rested with the pilots of the newly created Royal Naval Air Service. In order to undertake this task a number of airfields were set up and each had a flight of aircraft attached. One such airfield was Eastchurch, on the Isle of Sheppey.

Although today an open prison, it is not difficult to visualise how this airfield must have looked in earlier years. Only a few buildings connected with this one time air station still remain, but, on the other hand, the site is still open, and the lush green grass, for which the airfield was noted, still grows. On one side of the airfield there is a shallow hill which, in the years before World War One, was used by the famous C. S. Rolls in a number of gliding experiments. The nearby roads are named after aviation pioneers, whilst on the approach road to the airfield there is a memorial to the early pioneers of flight.

Eastchurch, in fact, has a long and fruitful association with flying. It started life as an airfield in 1910, when this rather low lying area was leased to the Royal Aero Club. In their hands it rapidly became a focal point for the early aviators, and was used by such pioneers as Brabazon, Sopwith and Rolls.

The airfield's connection with military flying dates to April 1911 when the first of many Royal Navy personnel arrived at the airfield in order to train as pilots. A few months before this the Aero Club had made an offer to the navy in which, for a period of six months, they allowed the senior service free use of the airfield together with an aeroplane and instructor. Out of that public spirited offer there was later to emerge the Royal Naval Air Service. Once the initial six months had passed, the navy took up a lease on one part of the airfield, and established the first naval flying school.

With the approach of war, the importance of Eastchurch greatly increased. As part of the permanent naval establishment, it became one of a ring of coastal air stations protecting various naval establishments. This was in 1912 and, at the time, it was difficult to see just how Eastchurch was supposed to perform this duty, when there was not one single aeroplane stationed there capable of carrying weapons. Even by August 1914 the number of armed aeroplanes had only risen to two.

During the early years of World War One, there was no officially organised defence system. Those naval aircraft ready to combat the Zeppelin threat were eventually armed, but nothing appeared to be standardized. Some had machine guns, some the 'Hayles' anti-Zeppelin grenade whilst others even converted smooth bore shot guns, Webley revolvers or anything else that came to hand.

Crew of a Gotha are buried in Margate Cemetery, after crashing at Manston on August 22nd 1917 (A.H. Simnison)

Manston from the air (East Camp) June 1916 (Geoff. Williams)

The aircraft, too, were a bit of a motley collection, consisting of Avro 504 trainers, Be 2 reconnaissance types and a few Martinsydes and Bristol Scouts.

For Kent, the first actual air raid occurred on Christmas Eve, 1914. On this occasion, one German seaplane managed to drop two bombs close to the Admiralty pier at Dover. On Christmas Day, itself, a further raid took place, this time when a Taube unloaded a bomb close to the railway station in the small North Kent village of Cliffe. At the time, these events were fairly dramatic, but causing no injury, or damage, they were as nothing when compared with the pointless devastation which was yet to come.

When an air raid did occur, the nearest airfields were notified by telephone, and the duty pilots would take-off. They would be armed with, perhaps, some vague grid reference and their only hope of finding the enemy relied upon him remaining on a straight flight. Sometimes, though, the attacking aircraft might appear over an airfield. Should such an event occur, then there was one mad dash as every aeroplane was scrambled. Some would be no more than training types, and would certainly not have the power, or armament, for tackling such an opponent.

During 1915 and 1916, Zeppelins would use the straights of Dover as a navigational aid. Flying towards the coast of Kent, they would pick out a suitable land mark, and then set course for London. Sometimes they dropped their bombs 'en route', and these would frequently fall in open fields, or upon isolated farms. However, in 1916, much of this changed when a series of more intensive attacks were carried out upon London, and certain other targets such as Sheerness, Ramsgate and Dover. The defences seemed hopelessly incapable of dealing with the situation as, time after time, the Zeppelins got through.

The nation's defences were re-structured. The Royal Flying Corps was given the task of defending the country. A series of new squadrons were formed, with one of them, number 50, based at Dover, but with flights detached to Bekesbourne and Throwley. The Zeppelins now began to meet their match. The Flying Corps, using fast anti-Zeppelin fighters, and co-operating with increasing numbers of anti-aircraft guns, started to make life very difficult for the airship. At first the Germans simply changed their tactics. They started to fly by night, but even this proved rather hazardous. Eventually they turned away from the airship and started to rely upon huge twin engined bombers.

Towards the beginning of the war the Germans had established an airfield at Ostende, the purpose of which was to mount air raids upon England. All this, however, proved rather ineffectual as the range of these early bombers was restricted. However, by 1917 a new long range bomber aircraft had been developed by the Gotha Wagonfabrik Works. These aircraft were introduced into squadron service during the winter of 1916 and, before long, a series of new airfields had been established in the Ghent area.

Raids with these new bombers were started on May 25th, 1917. It was a daylight operation, with the German bombers much hindered by cloud. Unable to locate London, they finally arrived over Folkestone, where a number of

Captured Albatross, Manston 1917,   (Geoff. Williams)

Manston, March 1916.   (Geoff Williams)

aircraft subsequently jettisoned their bomb load. Perhaps their target had been the military camp at Shorncliffe, or even the harbour, but the bombs actually fell into the crowded shopping centre. The result was a horrible, bloody, massacre. Ninety-seven shoppers were killed, a further 114 were injured, and the latest weapon of war proved its ability to destroy a defenceless target.

Following this raid, there was a public outcry. More squadrons had to be brought back from France, with 56 squadron arriving at Bekesbourne on 5th July. The squadron remained there for two weeks, receiving a number of false alarms, but never coming into contact with the enemy. The day after they returned to France a further major air raid occurred.

Attacks by Gotha and the larger 'R' class Giant bombers followed throughout the autumn and winter of 1917. Kentish towns received bombs whenever the attacker was thwarted from reaching London. But daylight raids presented the Germans with a number of problems. The defences, which had continued to be strengthened, started to take their toll. Bomber losses gradually mounted until a decision was taken to implement night raids. The first of these was carried out on September 3, 1917 when four Gotha bombers attacked Margate, Sheerness and Chatham. Whereas damage to both Margate and Sheerness was negligible, this was far from the case at Chatham. One bomb, dropped by the leading aeroplane, fell into the naval barracks. It hit the gymnasium, which was then acting as a dormitory, and killed a huge number of naval ratings. In fact, this one bomb, which was responsible for causing the deaths of 136 individuals, caused more loss of life than any other bomb during that entire war.

Other night raids followed. Before the end of September Cliftonville and Margate were subjected to the attention of Gotha bombers. Both towns suffered heavy civilian casualties. Not surprisingly, many of these Kent towns were given a ring of anti-aircraft guns together with numerous searchlight emplacements. In addition to all this, London received a huge curtain of barrage balloons which protected the capital with a forest of cables suspended between balloons. It was hoped that this would force the bombers to fly higher. Perhaps it did. Though one bomber, an R.12, a five engined monstrosity, actually flew into the 'balloon apron' and still survived.

Hastily developed night fighters were brought into service. Usually they were adaptations of existing aircraft then being used for day time defence. These included the Sopwith Camel and the Be 2c. More airfields were also established and, in Kent, these included Wye, Penshurst, Leigh, Grove Park and Ash Green. Conditions at these airfields were somewhat primitive and goose neck paraffin flares were the main landing aid. Searchlights were also used to illuminate the landing grounds, but these often had the unfortunate effect of blinding the pilot and causing a fatal crash.

Two other airfields used in the war against the Gothas were those of Detling and Manston. Both originally started out as naval air stations, though Detling was handed over to the Royal Flying Corps in early 1917. Manston, originally

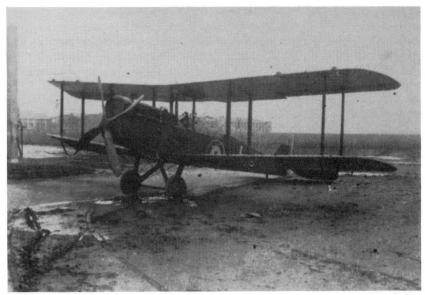

De Havilland D.H.4 '1' at Hawkinge (F. Young)

Sopwith Dolphin, possibly awaiting disposal, at Hawkinge shortly after World War One.
(F. Young)

an emergency landing ground, became part of the home defences when, in April 1916, a squadron was permanently stationed there. A nearby farmhouse became the officers' mess, whilst a number of other buildings were also requisitioned. Plans to form a Handley Page bomber squadron at Manston were considered, but nothing came to fruition. However, in December 1916 a Handley Page training school was formed there, acting as a feeder unit for squadrons in France. With the increase of Gotha raids on London, Manston's fighter force was increased when all naval aircraft stationed at Detling were transferred to Manston.

A major problem in combatting the earliest German air raids was exactly how a fighter was expected to locate its target. For this an improved method of reporting the progress of enemy aircraft was adopted. The result was the forma-tion of an embryo observer corps, in the form of regular and special police constables. Their duties consisted of keeping a watch for enemy aircraft and immediately phoning the nearest sector control. This way an aeroplane's position could be constantly charted as it flew over each of the areas covered by these constables. This information, together with its regular up-dating, was transmitted to airborne home defence fighters by means of flashing searchlights or, in day-light, huge white arrows placed on the ground.

Despite all this, raids on Kent continued. Many of them, however, were accidental as the real target was London. Gothas, though, were prone to engine failure, and it was common for them to jettison bomb loads to facilitate a quick return passage. Not that this always worked. On the night of December 19th, 1917, a Gotha with obvious engine trouble, flew low over Margate. Skimming the roof tops it landed in a field near Westfield Road, Garlinge. The crew promptly set it alight before surrendering to the police. Next day German machine guns were found at Grosvenor Place and Twenties Farm, presumably jettisoned from the strickened aircraft in a bid to lighten its load.

The night raiders' last fling came on the night of May 19/20, 1918, when no less than forty-two aircraft, mostly Gothas, took part in a raid on London. As on so many previous occasions, bombs were also dropped on Margate, Faversham and Dover. On their way back, however, these bombers were given a severe mauling by the defences. Both anti-aircraft fire, and home defence fighters took their toll of the German aircraft. In all, four enemy aircraft were brought down. For the raiders, this was the end of the war. They were never again to return in such force.

Amongst the Battle of Britain airfields which have so far remained unmen-tioned are those of Hawkinge, Lympne and Biggin Hill. This is due to their limited connection with the air defence role in this earlier period. Biggin Hill, admittedly, did have a fighter squadron attached to it. but this was not until December 1917, and made this airfield rather a late comer. At the time, Biggin Hill was more heavily engaged in experimental work, and the addition of a squadron there was, if anything, a side show. Hawkinge and Lympne, on the other hand, were repair and refuelling depots used by aircraft being delivered to France.

King's Birthday Parade on Sports Ground, Manston, 1937. Acacia Cafe and Margate road on left. (W.L. Grout)

Biggin Hill's experimental role was in developing ground-to-air radio communications. Here the Wireless Testing Park was established, with endless experiments being carried out on every aspect of radio communication. Pairs of aircraft would leave the airfield and head out for the continent, trying to maintain radio contact at all times. Progress was slow. Old equipment had to be up-dated, new equipment adapted and future equipment designed. It was not a particularly enviable task, but it was a vital component for all future military flying.

With the armistice came a reduction in the previously high level of defence spending. The newly created Royal Air Force suffered particularly heavy cutbacks, with a number of airfields being closed. Among the Kent airfields retained by the RAF were those of Biggin Hill, Eastchurch, Hawkinge and Manston. Lympne, on the other hand, saw only commercial flying during this inter-war period, whilst Detling was among those shut down.

Lympne, in fact, became the home of the world famous 'Cinque Ports Flying Club'. Here commercial aviation was carefully fostered by such events as the Light Aeroplane Trials held during the 1920s. Lympne was also a customs check point during these years, and responsible for the clearance of inward and outward bound flights. At this airfield, aircraft about to cross the Channel would have to land and obtain clearance before proceeding. Being close to the French coast, Lympne was frequently used by the pioneers of long distance flight. Many famous personalities of early aviation passed through Lympne on record breaking flights to Africa, The Cape, Australia and New Zealand.

Hawkinge, retained by a much diminished Royal Air Force, housed, at one time, the only fighter defence squadron in the country. This was twenty-five squadron which was based at Hawkinge for a good many years. It was equipped with a succession of front line fighters, culminating in the delightful Hawker Fury. Using this particular aeroplane the squadron was responsible for a number of thrilling aerobatic displays at the ever popular Hendon Air Pageants.

At the end of World War One, Hawkinge had become the holding aerodrome for redundant aircraft, with vast numbers of fighter and bomber aircraft being held there until broken-up, or otherwise disposed of. No. 2 Army Co-Operation squadron also found residence at Hawkinge, moving there from Manston. Much of their time was spent in the training of observers on a 'Haskgard Target'. This consisted of a large table top model of a typical terrain. Beneath this an 'erk' would crawl, and then proceed to puff cigarette smoke through a series of holes, so simulating shell and bomb bursts. These, the trainee observers would carefully plot. This, perhaps, is the only time that smoking on parade was officially allowed!

Another airfield rapidly run down during this period was Eastchurch. In 1923, No. 207 squadron, flying DH 9As was based there for a short period. But this was about the only squadron which remained at Eastchurch on anything like a permanent basis. For most of the period, the airfield witnessed the numerous comings and goings of squadrons using the nearby firing range at Leysdown. Immediately after the cessation of hostilities a number of squadrons had been transferred to Eastchurch but only for purposes of disbandment. In April 1922 an Armament Gunnery School was established at Eastchurch, and this took responsibility for training pilots in the use of aerial weapons. At this time, the main aircraft in use by the Gunnery School was the Westland Wapiti and the Hawker Hart.

Manston, although reduced somewhat severely from its wartime establishment, continued to train numerous RAF personnel. Indeed, it became a major centre for the training of aircraft fitters and riggers, being designated No. 1 School of Technical Training. Also finding a home at Manston during this period were a number of Army Co-Operation and Bomber squadrons. In 1933, the airfield became the home of No. 500, County of Kent, auxiliary squadron. Equipped initially with Vickers Virginias, it later received the Hawker Hart and then the Anson. As part of the Royal Auxiliary Air Force, its members were frequently dubbed as the 'weekend flyers' and 'the glamour boys', yet they were more than to prove themselves during the war time years.

Biggin Hill was retained for some time as an experimental base for wireless communication. It was also the location for experiments with 'sound mirrors', by which aircraft were detected as a result of engine noise. A large parabolic

Manston Airfield, June 1930. A large number of private aircraft appear in the foreground brought there by a specially laid on garden party. Life was hectic in those days!
('Flight' Magazine Neg. No. 8950)

Lympne Airfield, August 1930. The third hangar to the right belonged to the Cinque Ports Flying Club. 601 (County of London) Squadron are in residence, using the Wapiti Bomber
('Flight' Neg. No. 4068)

Biggin Hill, Empire Day 1935. Bristol Bulldogs, 32 (F) Squadron (A. Boorman)

mirror, mounted on gimbals, was built on the North Downs and adjacent to the aerodrome. Experiments were then carried out to establish whether aircraft formations could be tracked using this method. It was partially successful with the slow flying bombers of that period, and plans were drawn up for a chain of similar mirrors to be built along the south and east coasts. Later developments in engine power and aircraft speed, combined with failures to eliminate extraneous noises such as waves, wind and even sea gulls, rendered them obsolete before the complete chain was constructed. The fiction of 'sound detection', however, was promoted right up to World War Two, as a cover story for the infant radar system. A further development of sound was the use of the Biggin Hill mirror as a source rather than a receiver of sound. A klaxon was mounted on the mirror, emitting a stream of noises, and designed to help pilots locate the aerodrome in bad weather, or at night. Unfortunately, the high pitched sound resulted in numerous broken windows and stampeding cattle. It was eventually demolished after several aircraft flew into the mirror during foggy weather.

Like Hawkinge, Biggin Hill became a fighter station and various squadrons were based there. Amongst these were 56, 23, 32, 79 having regular changes of equipment, from Sopwith Snipes, Gloster Grebes, Gamecocks to Hawker Demons, Bristol Bulldogs, and Gloster Gauntlets. A Night Flying and an Anti-Aircraft co-operation flight had its base at Biggin Hill, equipped with Vickers Vimys, then Hawker Horsleys and Westland Wallaces.

Biggin Hill. Gloster Gauntlets of 32 Squadron, Empire Air Day 1937 (F.G. Evans)

Rebuilt Control Tower at Gravesend Airport. (P. Connolly)

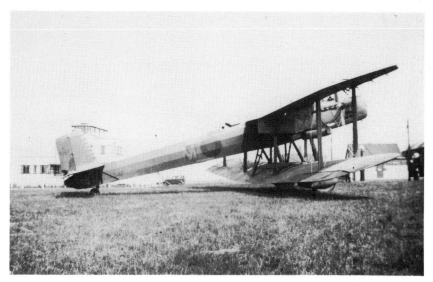

K.5197 Handley Page Heyford III of 99 Squadron (Mildenhall) at Gravesend 1938
(S. Parsonson)

As an RAF station Detling was not re-opened until the late 1930s. At that point it was attached to No. 16 Group Coastal Command, with No. 500 squadron being transferred there from Manston. By then, this squadron had been re-equipped with the Anson, and was soon to play an important role in reconnaissance operations carried out over the Channel.

Two further airfields, Gravesend and West Malling, have so far remained unmentioned. Both, in fact, were established during the inter-war years. It was in 1932 that the private limited company of Gravesend Aviation was formed with the aim of establishing an airfield at Thong Lane, Chalk. Work quickly progressed, and in October of that year Gravesend Airport was officially opened. For the occasion the National Aviation Air Days display team under its leader, Sir Alan Cobham visited the airport and gave a series of demonstrations. Also on display was an autogiro built to the design of the Spaniard, Cierva, by the Avro Company.

The airport at Gravesend had been built strictly for commercial purposes and, for this reason, it adopted the name of Gravesend-London (East). For a number of years it flourished, seeing the establishment of the Percival Aircraft Company. This company was responsible for building a number of light, high speed aircraft, which were used in several long distance record breaking flights. To demonstrate how good his products were, Mr Edgar Percival flew his Mew Gull to Oran in Algeria and back in one day. Also at Gravesend a flying club was established, an

K.7032 Handley Page Harrow 41 of R.A.E. at Gravesend 1938 (flown in by Alec Clouston)
(S. Parsonson)

Maidstone Airport Opening Ceremony Vickers Virginias 500 Squadron fly overhead
(F. Evans)

Gloster Gamecock at Eastchurch during the 1930's. A great number of squadrons visited the airfield for gunnery practice.

air taxi and charter firm was set up and the firm of Essex Aero moved in to establish themselves as masters of overhaul and tuning of racing and record breaking aircraft. One such was a D.H. 88 Comet which took part in the London to Melbourne air race. This particular aircraft, G-ACSS, was subsequently discovered, during 1941, under tarpaulin outside the main hangar. It was completely forgotten about until refurbished for the Festival of Britain. It is now being restored by the Shuttleworth trust.

West Malling, originally Maidstone Airport, dates to 1930. Like Gravesend it was a commercial venture established by a private company. At this time, of course, the airfield was no more than a collection of huts with a clubhouse in one corner. Later the airfield was adopted by C. H. Lowe-Wylde, often called the father of gliding in Kent. He built several BAC (British Aircraft Company) gliders in a disused laundry situated close to the airfield. Later he moved to premises situated behind the 'Nags Head' in Maidstone. The airfield became known as West Malling in 1935 when it was taken over by the Malling Aviation Company, and remained in their hands until 1938. In that year West Malling, in common with a number of airfields up and down the country, fell into the hands of the RAF. War was just over the horizon.

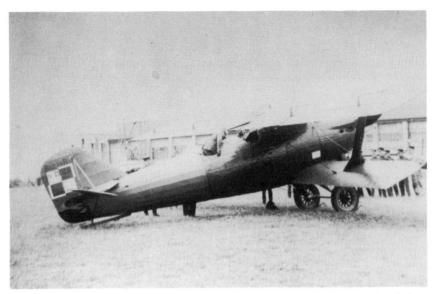

A Polish Breguet, No. 1128, at Eastchurch in 1931. It was not unusual for aircraft from various European Air Forces to visit RAF stations in this period (S.A. Johnson)

Armstrong-Whitworth Siskin 111A at Eastchurch during the 1930's.

It was the Munich crisis of September 1938 which first put the nation on a war time footing. The Royal Air Force, for its part, hastily daubed its aircraft with camouflage paint and colourful squadron markings now disappeared. The training of pilots became a priority as a number of Elementary Reserve Flying Training Schools were established. In this particular organization civilian reservists, preparing for call up, could complete their preliminary training during weekends and the late summer evenings. At Rochester, a factory airfield leased by Short Brothers, No. 23 ERFTS was formed.

With the outbreak of war during the early autumn of 1939, several changes were witnessed by those various airfields located throughout the county of Kent. New squadrons began to arrive, whilst the pace of life markedly increased. At Rochester, the EFTS unit was hastily transferred to Belfast, whilst Manston lost its training squadrons and Technical Training School.

During the early months of World War Two Eastchurch took on a slightly more unusual role. It became the receiving station for members of the Polish Air Force who wished to continue the fight against Germany. The first batch of Poles arrived from France on December 8th, 1939 and by March of the following year there were nearly 1,300 Poles stationed there. A number were dispatched to the Elementary Flying Training Schools, whilst others were formed into separate units. However, in May 1940, with the pace of war beginning to increase, the Polish contingents were moved to Blackpool. This Polish interlude did cause a few problems, as the Polish airmen seemed somewhat less disciplined than their RAF counterparts. The result was that many local residents tell of how uniformed Polish officers would often be seen arm in arm with the most questionable of female company. Moreover, the standard of driving by the Poles left something to be desired as these airmen, in their newly acquired fast cars, would speed along the narrow English lanes in the most 'devil may care' fashion.

No sooner had things begun to settle at the various Kent airfields than Germany invaded the Low Countries. Almost as rapidly, numerous RAF squadrons were directed abroad. As part of the Advanced Air Striking Force, these squadrons used many of the Kent airfields as staging posts. Within a few months the whole process was reversed, and these squadrons returned, and usually via the same Kent airfields.

During the evacuation of Dunkirk only the most sporadic of fighter cover could be provided. Of the Kent airfields, Manston, Hawkinge and Lympne were the ones most heavily used for this task. Other stations, further inland, used these airfields for re-fuelling and re-arming. For the RAF, these dark days which Dunkirk epitomizes, were far from memorable. The troops on the ground felt they merited far greater air cover. The pilots of Fighter Command might well have agreed, but the orders came from much higher up. The RAF must, at all costs, preserve its resources. To throw huge numbers of fighters into the battle at this point would have been suicidal. Spitfires and Hurricanes were far too precious a commodity. Only six weeks after Dunkirk they, together with the Fighter Command airfields in Kent, were all that stood between Hitler and total victory. The Battle of Britain was about to begin.

Biggin Hill 1940. Group Captain Grice congratulates three WAAF's on their military medals. Left to right: Sgt Jean Mortimer, Cpl Elspeth Candlish-Henderson, Sgt Emily Turner.
(Imperial War Museum)

Unveiling War Memorial Biggin Hill circa 1922. Buildings of South Camp, Biggin Hill Aerodrome in background. Colonel Blandy, D.S.O., former O/C Biggin Hill, Wireless Experimental Establishment (left) performed the ceremony.
(L. Nelson)

Chapter Three
BIGGIN HILL

By Len Pilkington

So much has already been written about Biggin Hill, that when the Battle of Britain is mentioned this most famous of all fighter stations immediately springs to mind. No book on Kentish Battle of Britain airfields would be complete without the story of Biggin Hill related by a few people who knew the fighter station at the time.

It was the most important of the Kentish airfields because it was the Sector or Controlling station having a satellite airfield at West Malling and forward fields at Hawkinge and Lympne (Ashford). Two other Kentish fighter airfields, those of Gravesend and Manston were often used by Biggin Hill's aircraft, but were technically controlled by Hornchurch. Also, to fool the Germans, Biggin Hill had a dummy or decoy airfield seven miles to the East North East at Lullingstone — a prewar site for a proposed London Airport. But the Luftwaffe knew all about it and had it marked on their target maps.

Biggin Hill, part of the No. 11 Group Fighter Command, with headquarters at Uxbridge, formed one of a ring with other Sector airfields around London, Kenley to the west, Hornchurch and North Weald to the north, and Northolt to the north west. Geographically, Biggin Hill was a fairly remote country station, 600 ft. above sea level, perched on the Downs between Bromley and Westerham, accessible only by the 410 Country Bus service, or car.

My first impressions of Biggin Hill, as a lad just prior to the war, were of narrow leafy lanes and gleaming silver aeroplanes in the hangars which skirted the road. It was a station cricket match, on a pitch where now stands the civil airport. A hot summer's day, of long grass and tall dog daisies, with strawberries from the adjoining farms for tea, served in one of the South Camp messes.

The airfield of course was to grow over the years, and was to become a motley collection of buildings of varying architectural styles concentrated in two main areas. The older site, adjacent to Biggin Hill village, South Camp, set up as a radio site in 1917 had strong army connections. Consisting of married quarters, a school of Anti-Aircraft Defence, a Searchlight Experimental Establishment, Motor Transport Sheds and an important Power Station, it stood on the site which is now the entrance to the civil airport. The other site or North Camp. the Leaves Green end of the airfield, had some buildings dating back to the early days but was developed mainly in the 1929-31 airfield expansion scheme.

The road from the 'King's Arms', Leaves Green, going towards Biggin Hill soon curves and runs through the buildings of the North Camp. On the left hand side of the road, behind the iron railings, were the modern barrack blocks and messes and further round the curve was the Main Gate. Directly opposite and on the other side of the road were the married quarters. Rounding the curve, past

Biggin Hill
Flugplatz

Länge (ostw. Greenw.): 0° 02″   Nördl. Breite: 51° 19′ 30″
Zielhöhe über NN 177 m

Maßstab etwa: 1 : 18 500

Lfl. Kdo. 3   Juli 1941

Karte 1 : 100 000
GB / E 34 b / d

GB 10 17 Biggin Hill, Flugplaß   750 × 1200 m
1. 2 Startbahnen, 750 u. 850 m lang
2. 7 Hallen
3. Unterkunfts- und Nebengebäude

bebaute Fläche

etwa 15 200 qm
etwa 19 800 qm

etwa 35 000 qm

4. Splitterschutzstände für Flugzeuge
5. Flakstellungen

Gleisanschluß nicht vorhanden

Biggin Hill 2.9.1940. The airfield camouflage and filled in bomb craters can be seen.
(Christopher R. Elliott)

50

A pair of Biggin Hill's 79 Squadron Hurricane 1's 1939 (S. Parsonson)

the Main Gate, was the original hangar, built around 1918 and in the typical RAF style of the time, of three bays and the classical bow string type roof. Next and fronting the road was the Station Headquarters, a brick built building with a pitched roof set off with an attractive cupola. Directly opposite, and again on the other side of the road, was the vital Sector Operations Block, well remembered by Leading Aircraftman (L.A.C.) E. D. Williams who, in 1938, cycled every Thursday evening from London for RAFVR training in the operations room. L.A.C. E. D. Williams was called up during the Munich crisis of 1938. Released after the crisis had passed but called up again in 1939, he served at Biggin Hill until 1942 when he was posted overseas.

Following on the line of buildings, hugging the road and opposite Salt Box Hill, was a tall pitched roof hangar with gable ends, rather austere and untypical of the 1930's RAF architectural style. It was steel framed with concrete infil, high windows and offices built onto the side wall. On the far corner of this hangar was the strange sugar loaf shaped building — 'The Salt Box Cafe'. This gave its name to the hill opposite, and had been resident there since the 1880's, long before the airfield was thought of. Finally, before the South Camp was reached, was the third hangar, single bay and of the Belfast type.

It was the division of the North Camp and the close proximity of hangars and other vital installations to the road which posed quite a security problem and led to the closure of the road when war was declared. The only route past the airfield for civilians was by special bus and Mr J. S. Nelson, of the Bromley Local History Society, remembers as a lad the amended service:

"One would take the 410 bus from Bromley and alight at the 'King's Arms', Leaves Green. Passengers would then board a single decker bus with blacked out windows and an armed guard and proceed past the airfield to be deposited at the 'Black Horse', Biggin Hill, there to take another 410 bus and continue the journey to Biggin Hill Village and Westerham, and vice versa if travelling the other way."

Wing Commander I.H. Cosby who flew with 610 and 72 Squadrons during the Battle of Britain. (I.H. Cosby)

WAAF Corporal D. Finnie who served in the Operations Room during the Battle of Britain.

Biggin Hill, 1939. The last Empire Air Display before the war. Hurricane 1's of 79 Squadron run up in front of the triple bay hangar. The cupola of the station Headquarters can be seen in the background (Kent Messenger)

The first months of the war were very quiet and called the 'phoney war' by the newspapers. 1940 opened with a severely cold winter, one of the worst for many years. WAAF Corporal Mrs D. Finnie was posted to Biggin Hill in 1940 as an Aircraftwoman (AC/W) for operations duties after volunteering for special duties whilst at Uxbridge. She was one of the first WAAFs in operations at Biggin Hill, and remembers very well the huge drifts of snow blocking the airfield and roads, and the inadequate WAAF uniforms at the time, and how they were supplemented by an issue of Airmen's greatcoats.

The bad weather in England and Europe restricted operations for the Blenheims of 610 Squadron and the Mark One Hurricanes of 32 and 79 Squadrons based at Biggin Hill. 32 Squadron flew some shipping patrols, but activity was low until on 10th May 1940 the German armies invaded the Low Countries and the 'phoney war' had ended.

The German forces raced across Belgium, France and Holland and with it the air fighting began in earnest. The Hurricanes of 79 Squadron had been sent to France and were soon in action. 32 Squadron Hurricanes, now joined by the first Spitfires to operate from Biggin Hill, those of 610 Squadron, backed up the air fighting by daily sorties from Biggin Hill.

Within two weeks the Low Countries and France had been overrun, RAF Squadrons had been decimated in the air and on the ground. RAF personnel were returning to the UK by any route possible and 79 Squadron, whose Hurricanes had been destroyed on the ground, were back at Biggin Hill. During this time Biggin Hill received hundreds of RAF personnel evacuated from across the Channel, ferried in by RAF transports.

The fighting in France culminated in the evacuation of the trapped British Expeditionary Force at Dunkirk. Codenamed 'Operation Dynamo' it commenced on 26th May, 1940, and Hurricanes of 213 and 242 Squadron replacing 32 and 79 Squadrons, ordered away for a rest, flew endless patrols over the beaches. 229 Squadron, replacing 610 Squadron Spitfires, now moved to Gravesend and concentrated on home defence.

By 4th June Operation Dynamo was complete and the British Expeditionary Force were home. It was now a time for taking stock. Both sides had problems but of different kinds. The Allies had lost men and material whilst, for the enemy, its advance had been so swift that in many cases it had outrun its supplies.

For Britain, now alone, it was time to consolidate what forces remained, and prepare for a further onslaught. Aircraft production was stepped up, but the real problem was the shortage of experienced pilots. Much regrouping was done and pilots from other spheres of operation were converted to fighters. Wing Commander Cosby, soon to be flying from Biggin Hill, relates that after returning to the UK in May 1940 he was re-equipped with Army Co-operation Lysanders at Hooten Park and flew anti-invasion patrols, but the Air Ministry, looking for more experienced pilots with squadron service, called for volunteers to convert to fighters. The army, to all intents and purposes, were temporarily out of the battle and volunteers were therefore called for from the four Army Co-operation Squadrons in the UK:

An aerial photograph taken during the early stages of attack on the airfield, with German markings indicating bomb damage and damaged installations

1. Bomb explosions
2. Hangars
3. Assembly shops
4. Store houses
5. Repair shops & store houses
6. Workshop
7. Briefing hall
8. Barrack huts
9. Power station
10. Administration block
11. Dispersed aircraft

Biggin Hill, August 1940. Luftwaffe aerial photo of one of the early raids on the airfield, the camouflage marking to the landing area can be clearly seen   (Lashenden Air Warfare Museum)

"Conversion to fighters was at the Spitfire OCU Howarden near Chester and after a short briefing on the Spitfire, training commenced. There were no dual aircraft and we sat in the cockpit to familiarise ourselves with the layout, were given a pat on the head, told not to b— kill ourselves, wished the best of luck and launched into space.

"The Spitfire is a beautiful aircraft to fly but on its first meeting is formidable! The undercarriage is narrow making it appear unstable on the rough grass airfields at the time. Immediately in front of the pilot's face is the gunsight which at first seems to obstruct the whole of the view through the small bulletproof windscreen, and ahead of that a very long nose housing the 1030 HP Rolls Royce Merlin engine. The propellor being long requires a lot of ground clearance. Thus, whilst on the ground, the aircraft has a marked nose-up attitude, there is no forward vision when taxying (unless looking over the side with the hood open, which we did for take off and landing).

"My first take off was, therefore, quite an adventure and I found myself roaring across the airfield at about 140 mph with the airspeed rising alarmingly. I remembered the undercarriage to be selected 'UP'. It came up with quite a thump. It was the first time in my life I had ever retracted an undercarriage.

"We flew all day for six days, doing battle climbs and formation flying and I fired the guns only once off the coast of the Wirral. Some training!"

During Dunkirk all leave had been stopped at Biggin Hill, and in the hot weather of June preparations for the coming battle were begun. Security was tightened, and this included stopping completely the bus service which ran past the airfield, adding further hardships to the civilians of Biggin Hill.

Mr Nelson recalls that the bus service now had to run around the narrow lanes at the back of the airfield and to achieve this two narrow buses were employed. They would start together, one at the 'Black Horse' and proceed down Jail Lane, the other from the 'King's Arms' down Milking Lane, their timing to coincide at a wide passing point in the narrow lane at the back of the airfield. The camouflage of the airfield was altered and this is clearly visible on German target maps and aerial photographs, where hedges and ditches have been painted on the grass and runways with heavy oil or bitumen to correspond to natural colours, splitting the airfield into smaller units.

Captain D. Goodchild, Royal Artillery, was an NCO in the Territorial Army before the war. 34th Battalion, Queen's Own Royal West Kent Regiment, called up in the Munich Crisis and again in July 1939 to Biggin Hill. He remembers the strengthening of the Anti Aircraft defences at Biggin Hill. Additional 40 mm Bofors light Anti Aircraft guns were installed along with lighter Hispano-Suiza cannon and Lewis machine guns. Units of the Queen's Regiment were used for ground defences.

Captain Goodchild served in the vitally important Operations Block as an NCO and remembers "the Operations Block was above ground directly opposite and across the road from the Station Headquarters, about 80-100 ft. square,

Biggin Hill, 1940. The station Headquarters and gable ended hangar showing damage after an early raid on the airfield. It is believed the hole in the roof of the hangar was caused by a motor car blown into the air by a bomb and falling through the roof. The hangar was subsequently destroyed in a later raid except for parts of the outside wall, a small section remaining today. The station Headquarters and railings still stand

(Air Vice Marshal J. Worrall)

surrounded by a blastwall leaving a walkway about five feet wide all round. The Operations Room inside the Operations Block was not very big and had a table with a map of Southern England and Biggin Hill 'C' Sector upon which the plots of enemy aircraft were made by WAAF plotters — about six plotters per watch under a WAAF NCO." 'C' Sector encompassed an area of Kent and Sussex from Biggin Hill to the South Foreland in the east, and from Biggin Hill to Eastbourne to the south.

There was also a vertical glass screen dividing the room upon which was superimposed a map of 'C' Sector where rubber suckers placed from behind the WAAF and RAF personnel plotted the 'Pipsqueak' bearings, supplied by the Direction Finding room, of our own aircraft. The table was quite large, and tilted at an angle to give the controllers, on the balcony, a clear view of the plots coming in from No. 11 Group, Operations Room. The controllers were RAF and Army personnel: the RAF controlled the sector aircraft whilst the Army passed information concerning approaching enemy raids to the A.A. guns and searchlights in 'C' Sector.

When the Biggin Hill controllers ordered aircraft to 'Scramble', it was the last link in a chain of events which began with the first blips on the screens of the Radar stations dotted around the coast. The blips, interpreted by the Radar stations, were reported to a Filter room at Fighter Command HQ, Bently Priory, as were the visual sightings from Observer Corps posts, via their HQ at Horsham.

The Filter room assessed the accuracy of the reports and, if thought to be genuine, passed the information to No. 11 Group HQ Control Room, Uxbridge. No. 11 Group, commanded by Air Vice Marshall Keith Park, would then select the appropriate sector to deal with the enemy raid.

Once selected the Sector Operations Room had direct R/T contact with its aircraft based either at the Sector aerodrome or its forward or Satellite stations.

The aircraft after 'scrambling' were steered — 'vectored', at the correct altitude — 'angels' for the best possible interception position, if time permitted. R/T communication was possible between aircraft and operation — Biggin Hill was code named 'Sapper ' — but it was not possible for pilots to continuously report their position (if known!). So plots were obtained from an automatic transmission from one aircraft in each squadron by directional finding stations. They fed in the positions to a D/F room in the Operations Block for transferring to the plotting tables. With these 'Pipsqueak' plots it was possible for the controllers to assess the relative positions of enemy aircraft and our own.

The aircraft, once scrambled, would follow 'Sapper' controller but were frequently at a disadvantage as Wing Commander Cosby explains:

"It would take all the time to interception to climb to engage the enemy aircraft and usually the fighters were above us. We were not experienced in manoeuvring large squadrons of aircraft in combat and usually had the advantage of height and sun. Moreover, as the UK is also north of the French airfields used by the Luftwaffe, the sun was most times in our eyes. We had, however, the advantage of greater time in the air and the psychological advantage of fighting most times over home territory."

Back up control room facilities existed at Biggin Hill. WAAF Officer Mrs D. Finnie relates: "The standby operations room was in a cobblers shop in Biggin Hill village but we had only black boards and chalk on which to record the plots. We worked shifts from 8am—1pm, 1pm—5pm, 5pm—8pm, 8pm—midnight and midnight to 8am."

There was a lull in the warm June/July whilst the enemy were preparing for the invasion of England. 32 Squadron Hurricanes, now uprated with constant speed propellers, returned to Biggin Hill and 610 Squadron Spitfires joined them replacing 79 Squadron. Defiants of 141 Squadron paid a brief visit for a few days whilst passing through to West Malling. They later encountered heavy losses operating from the forward airfield at Hawkinge.

On 10th July the respite was over and the overture to Eagle Day commenced. Large formations of enemy fighters and bombers attacked shipping in the Channel to draw the RAF into the air. The Hurricanes of 32 Squadron and Spitfires of 610 Squadron flew endless sorties from dawn to dusk. With sixteen hours of daylight this imposed immense strains on the pilots, and our friends at Biggin remember the grey and strained looks which showed on the faces of the airmen.

By 12th August the enemy had lost 286 aircraft for the loss of 150 of our

Empire Air Day, Biggin Hill 1935. Hawker Demons 23 Squadron in front of gable ended hangar on left hand and triple bay hangar on right, both destroyed in 1940. (F.G. Evans)

own, and it became apparent to the Luftwaffe that the RAF could not be destroyed by these tactics. Now, on the eve of Eagle Day the fighting entered another phase and the largest aerial fleet yet assembled switched its attack to the Radar stations, and the No. 11 Group airfields.

Manston, Lympne and Hawkinge were badly bombed and the Spitfires of 610 Squadron and the Hurricanes of 32 Squadron continued with their forward airfields badly damaged. Bomb craters and unexploded bombs created numerous hazards when landing. August 15th saw some of the heaviest fighting so far, with 1800 enemy aircraft thrown into attack, firstly with feints upon the north east of England, then back to the south. In the evening two waves of aircraft were plotted with one on course for Biggin Hill.

Spitfires from Biggin Hill's 610 Squadron completely routed the wave destined for their home airfield, but the other wave got through to bomb Croydon airfield. The losses of aircraft according to official sources was now 75 German and 34 of our own. At the time however, a total German loss of 182 aircraft was claimed.

On Sunday 18th August* three major air assaults against Southern England resulted in the loss of 69 German and 68 British aircraft totally destroyed with others damaged in the air or on the ground. On no other day during the Battle of Britain would either side suffer a greater number of aircraft put out of action.

One raid was to be a combined high and low level attack on Kenley to coincide with a high level attack on Biggin Hill by Bomber Geschwader No. 76 and Bomber Geschwader No. 1. The high level attack crossed the coast at Dover at 12.50pm at 12,000 ft, consisting of 40 BF.109's followed by 27 DO.17's and 20 ME.110's and JU.88's of Bomber Geschwader No. 76. Fifteen miles behind were

*The description of this day is based largely on 'The Battle of Britain — The Hardest Day, 18th August, 1940' by Alfred Price, published by Macdonald and Janes.

58

SCRAMBLE! Pilots race to their Mk.1 Hurricanes, against background of Belfast type hangar. Almost certainly Biggin Hill, 32 Squadron.   (Kent Messenger — The County Paper of Kent)

the 60 HE.111's of Bomber Geschwader No. 1, with 40 escorting Bf.109's bound for Biggin Hill. Fifty miles to the south-west nine DO.17's of the 9th Staffel Bomber Geschwader No. 76 were between Dieppe and Beachy Head skimming the waves at zero feet.

At 1.03pm the high level attack passed over Ashford following the Folkestone— Reigate railway pointing like a long finger to the targets. The railway, still used by pilots today as a visual navigational aid, was used by Lufthansa pilots only a short time before the Battle of Britain to guide them to the civic airport of Croydon.

At the same time the low level attack of the nine DO.17's crossed the coast at Beachy Head, picking up the railway at Newhaven and by some excellent low level map reading at roof top height picked their way via Burgess Hill to Bletchingly and finally swooped on Kenley at 1.22, dead on time. The high level attack was late and should have arrived at Biggin Hill and Kenley before the DO.17's; consequently the high level attack on Kenley was diverted to West Malling, but the raid on Biggin Hill continued.

At Biggin Hill the Hurricanes of 32 Squadron and the Spitfires of 610 Squadron sat on the ground waiting until about 1.15 when the plots showed a raid imminent. The aircraft were then scrambled to protect their base.

At 1.27 the sixty HE.111's of Bomber Geschwader No. 1, stepped up at between 12,000 and 15,000 ft, were running in to bomb Biggin Hill, escorted by 40 Bf.109's from Fighter Geschwader No. 54.

The only heavy A.A. unit, part of the 58th Heavy A.A. Regiment was located just south of Biggin Hill equipped with four obsolete 3 inch guns holding fire initially because of British fighters overhead. As a result Bomber Geschwader No. 1 was allowed a clear run to find its target.

Most people at Biggin Hill had time to take cover and the majority of the attack fell on the landing ground and in the woods to the east. The Motor Transport buildings received a direct hit with two people killed and three wounded. The Operations room received some damage and the glass sector maps were broken. The sick quarters received some damage and Corporal Mumford, NCO in charge, was moved out and helped set up a new treatment centre in the decontamination centre, a much sturdier and better protected building.

Corporal Mumford also remembers the crew of a German bomber shot down in Leaves Green was brought to the Sick Quarters for treatment.

The task of cleaning up began. Craters had to be filled in for aircraft to take off and land but unexploded bombs added to the problem. One of the first military medals awarded to a member of the WAAF at Biggin Hill was won by Sergeant Joan Mortimore working in the armoury and later going round the airfield with red flags marking the unexploded bombs.

The weather now curtailed activities, but sporadic attacks continued. On Friday 30th August a large raid developed before noon on No. 11 Group Airfields but 79 Squadron Spitfires, back at Biggin Hill, along with 610 Squadron Spitfires, averted an attack on the airfield. However the raid caused much damage to Keston, Biggin Hill Village and surrounding areas.

About 6 o'clock that evening the Luftwaffe caught Biggin Hill unawares. On a beautiful summer's evening nine JU.88's flew at low level up the Ashford—Reigate railway swinging north to take Biggin Hill by complete surprise. 610 Squadron was away but 79 Squadron had returned and was sitting on the ground when the first bombs fell.

It was a meal time and people were caught off guard. The raid was short and sharp, but the damage wreaked was tremendous. Aircraft were damaged on the ground and most of the motor transport was destroyed. An air raid shelter was hit and there were many casualties.

Mr Nelson, with a few of his school chums, was up a tree in the village, their favourite vantage point, and he relates the event:

"It was a beautiful evening after a day of much activity. There had been fighting overhead all day. The sky had been full of the white criss-cross of the vapour trails and the noise had been continuous. The drone of the aero engines mingled with the sound of gunfire and the perpetual rain of bits falling out of the sky.

"At around six o'clock we saw a formation of about nine aircraft flying from the South South West very low and slow, following the Westerham Road, and silver in the evening light. It was not until we saw the first bombs leave the aircraft and the black crosses on the wings that we realised they were not a formation of our own Blenheims.

Biggin Hill, North Camp, after the bombing. Spitfires of 611 Squadron fly over narrow Bromley-Westerham Road, on 9.12.1942 running past North Camp buildings. Salt Box Cafe and remains of gable roofed hangar behind which can be seen the cupola of the station headquarters. In front a 40mm Bofors A.A. gun and nissen huts and sheds used for maintenance and dispersal.   (BBC Hulton Picture Library)

"There was a tremendous amount of noise from the airfield as the bombs exploded and the guns opened up. Some Spitfires got airborne and chased the raiders."

In the sick quarters, now occupying the decontamination centre, the casualties soon began to arrive. The situation was worsened by the fact that most essential services had been cut as soon as the first bombs fell.

Corporal Mumford remembers:

"after the first bomb fell the electric lighting failed and the emergency battery set was used. This failed also after the third or fourth bomb and torches were used to treat the ever growing list of casualties.

"The bombs had blocked the narrow main roads and the service roads inside the airfield and these had to be cleared before ambulances and help from Orpington could get through.

"At first RAF personnel started to clear the debris on the shelter until ARP rescue squads from Bromley could get through the blocked main road. Finally a team of Welsh miners arrived and the clearing operations were rapidly speeded up.

61

"The civilian rescue services from Orpington and Bromley were marvellous. The ARP and rescue squads would race to the airfield after each raid and three local doctors, Dr J. C. Colbeck, Dr Grant and Dr J. C. Mansi worked alongside the RAF personnel in the Sick Quarters and in rescue operations. Dr J. C. Colbeck for his trouble lost his car when a 1,000 kg bomb blew it through the roof of a hangar."

WAAF Corporal Mrs D. Finnie was in a truck, just passing the airfield, when the raid struck. "Suddenly bombs were falling and machine gun bullets strafed the ground. We all jumped out of the truck and landed in a nearby ditch. The raid was soon over but the damage was appalling."

The next day brought another raid and some had their lighter moments. L.A.C. Denis Gee recalls that about midday "I was in the main transmission station near the main gate with a whole crowd of airmen, some at the Salvation Army Canteen across the road, when German aircraft made a run across the airfield. We all made for the wood nearby and when the raid had finished I remembered shouting 'Parachutists!' Luckily I had mistaken the glint of the sun on the barrage balloons near Bromley!"

The raids were a great strain on all personnel and on none more than the maintenance and repair units. L.A.C. S. R. Roberts, an engine fitter, recalls the constant working into the late hours to keep the aircraft flying.

The next evening another low level attack, by a few aircraft flying out of the sun, reduced Biggin Hill to a shambles. Mr Nelson relates that the locals firmly believed that the white scars on the chalk escarpment at Woldingham were used by the Luftwaffe to take a bearing on the airfield. Club pilots know today that in good visibility once crossing the south coast and crossing the first line of downs, even at low altitudes the scars on the north downs or 'ridge' make good sightings for the airfields in the Redhill, Kenley, Biggin Hill area.

After the raid hardly a building had escaped damage and the vital operations had been hit and put out of action. Captain Goodchild, on duty at the time, remembers the evacuation to the Cobblers Shop in the village which now assumed the role of the main Operations Room.

Two further Military Medals were awarded to members of the WAAF for their gallantry during this raid, Sergeant Helen Turner and Corporal Elspeth Henderson, for manning the switchboards in the Operations Block until ordered to leave.

With so much damage to the buildings, the personnel of the airfield had to be dispersed to the surrounding villages. Mr Nelson remembers the billeting of RAF personnel in the village and in his own home. WAAF Corporal Mrs D. Finnie and AC/W Mrs Denis Gee were bombed out of their quarters and rehoused at 'The Cedars', Keston. The cookhouses were out of action and Mrs D. Gee was now cooking for the station in a nearby garage called 'Crossways'. Pilots were spread out in houses over a large area to reduce the risk of injury of bombing and Wing Commander Cosby was billeted in a large country house some miles from the airfield.

Wing Commander Cosby continues his narrative.

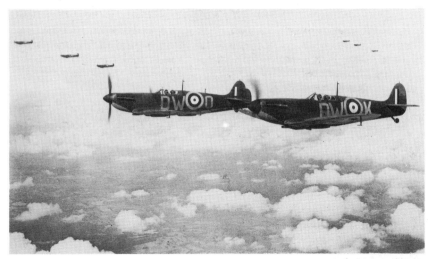

Spitfires of 610 'County of Chester' Squadron, Biggin Hill, July 1940 (Imperial War Museum)

"I was posted to Biggin Hill at the end of August with four others on a Monday morning to join 610 Squadron. I was just 21 years of age. Of the five of us I was the only one left by Friday, three others were killed and the fourth seriously injured.

"On joining 610 Squadron, the Adjutant asked to see my kit (one small bag, the rest had been lost in France) and instructed me to report to dispersal, a wooden hut on the eastern side of the airfield. There I met some of the aircrew and the Flight Commander, and drew a parachute. I received a good briefing and was told that I would not be needed until dawn next day.

"Dinner was in the No. 1 Officers Mess on the south side of the airfield (now demolished) and afterwards to the Squadron house some few miles from the camp. I never saw it in daylight as we were away before dawn and returned after dark.

"Next day at the airfield on a blackboard I was shown my position in the formation, allotted my aircraft, checked it over, put on my 'Mae West' and hoped for some breakfast. This arrived just as we were scrambled. The sortie was uneventful but on returning I hoped to eat my breakfast which had been delivered by the Squadron Humber Snipe shooting brake on trays from the mess. The congealed egg and bacon was now a sorry sight — I remember it well."

The raids continued and Graham Wallace in his book 'RAF Biggin Hill', describes how after the raid on 5th September Group Captain R. Grice, DFC,

63

the Station Commander, surveyed the damage from the air. He was obsessed with the idea that as long as any buildings looked intact the raids would continue. At 10,000 ft, from the station Magister, one hangar looked quite undamaged. He decided that to save further loss of life the hangar had to be destroyed. With the aid of some fellow officers and some explosive, what remained of the triple hangar disappeared with a loud bang.

This action was not looked on with approval by No. 11 Group, and whether this did influence the Luftwaffe was never determined but two days later on 7th September the Battle of Britain entered yet another phase, the attacks on the Sector Airfields was called off and the blitz on London began.

Meanwhile life at Biggin Hill had its lighter moments and West End bands would travel down in the evenings to entertain. Quite frequently the Windmill Girls would give a show in what was left of the buildings. The morale was never higher and the team spirit fantastic.

At the beginning of September 610 Squadron flew off to Acklington in the North East for a well earned rest and were replaced at Biggin Hill by 72 Squadron.

The beginning of the blitz on London I remember vividly. At Erith on the afternoon of Saturday, 7th September I watched with my father the battles three miles above. The sky was full of white contrails which soon were blotted out by two huge columns of black smoke rising from Woolwich to the west and from the burning oil storage tanks at Thameshaven to the east.

The raids continued by day and by night until on Sunday, 15th September, now remembered as Battle of Britain Day, came the climax with the Luftwaffe throwing everything into the battle. At Biggin Hill 92 Squadron led by Flight Lieutenant Brian Kingcombe now joined 72 Squadron, 79 Squadron moving away for a rest. On this day Fighter Command was stretched to the limit and every Squadron available was used in the furious and never ending storties.

After two weeks at Acklington, Wing Commander Cosby returned to Biggin Hill and joined 72 Squadron Spitfires and describes the style of air fighting: "One minute we were flying in a tight formation of twelve aircraft in which only the leader could see what was happening – the others fully employed keeping station. The next minute the whole formation broke up, each man for himself and we mixed in a gigantic ball of aircraft, some in flames, some spinning all at full throttle and then quite suddenly alone, without another aircraft in sight. My first victory came in September over the South Coast in such an encounter. I followed a Bf.109 down over Folkestone harbour putting him down in the sea just off the Mole. He went in with quite a splash. Notwithstanding this the pilot survived and was saved from drowning by an Army Officer who dived into the water and swam out to the wreck and pulled him ashore."

Hitler, realising the RAF could not be destroyed in this manner, postponed operation 'Sea Lion' two days later.

The raids however continued. To help with the night defences, Defiants of 141 Squadron paid a brief visit to Biggin Hill whilst 'en route' to Gatwick. In two consecutive nights they destroyed three enemy aircraft.

The Aerodrome, Biggin Hill, Kent.

Biggin Hill around 1925. The triple bay hangar was the first to be built in 1917 and destroyed in 1940. Local view published by Mr E. Wise. (Mr J. Wise)

There was a desperate shortage of pilots and Wing Commander Cosby recalls "soon the Squadron became decimated and hardly any of the pilots knew each other and the older ones needed a rest. 610 Squadron was sent off to Acklington in the North East to reform. It was the practice in these days for one of the Flight Commanders to become Squadron Commander, Deputy Flight Commander to become Flight Commander and the chaps who had been in for some time to become instructors to the new boys who went back as re-inforcements. After two weeks up north I returned to Biggin Hill with 72 Squadron."

In October Wing Commander Cosby left with 72 Squadron for Leconfield and 74 (Tiger) Squadron arrived. Their Commander was 'Sailor' Malan DFC, a man renowned for his 'Ten rules of Air Fighting', and later to become Station Commander at Biggin Hill.

With a deterioration in the weather, the style of war changed with single raiders providing nuisance value only. One such raid was described by L.A.C. Denis Gee: "A lone raider one morning approached the aerodrome out of cloud, circled two or three times, then dropped its bombs. The PAC rockets were fired but the aircraft disappeared into cloud."

The Battle of Britain officially ended on 31st October 1940 and the task of clearing up began. This was slow and as the year wore on the airfield became very muddy. Most of the units were still dispersed in the surrounding areas. The Operations Room, after a short spell in a Cobblers Shop moved to 'Towerfields',

65

Biggin Hill, South Camp 1959. Although taken after the war the remaining M.T. Sheds and Workshops can be seen, along with typical Aircraft Dispersal Pens   (Rex Nicholls)

Biggin Hill in 1979. Biggin Hill was to remain an RAF fighter station until January 1958 when it became the centre for aircrew selection. Still used by the Royal Air Force, Biggin Hill is now owned by Bromley Council.   (Len Pilkington)

a large house converted to Operations and Signals. Corporal Mumford moved with the Sick Quarters to Keston Guest Hotel. There were no hangars and few workshops, aircraft were parked and serviced in the armchair like blastpens at dispersal. L.A.C. Roberts remembers that all they had was a small shed in which to keep the trolley-acs for starting.

A good idea of what Biggin Hill looked like after the bombing can be seen in the photograph of Spitfires flying over the North Camp. Although taken in 1942 the remains of the Gable Hangar can be seen with the cupola of the Station Head-quarters proudly standing above it. To the left of the hangar remains is the strange shape of the Salt Box Cafe, whilst in front is a 40 mm Bofors A.A. gun. To the right, are the small sheds used by the maintenance units, and for aircraft dispersal.

In November Biggin Hill once again achieved fame when 74 Squadron's Flight Commander, J. C. Mungo-Park and H. M. Stephen, claimed the airfield's 600th enemy aircraft destroyed, and Biggin Hill became the first '600 station'. By December the tide was turning and before the end of 1940 Biggin Hill aircraft took the offensive with sweeps over France.

The RAF had won its most historic battle of all times and Biggin Hill had been part of it. Throughout the worst of the raids except for a few hours, it remained operational.

If one takes again the road from the 'King's Arms' to Biggin Hill there are reminders of the Battle. The Accommodation Blocks now bear the names of famous Battle of Britain Airfields and rounding the bend, past the old Decon-tamination Centre, a Spitfire and a Hurricane stand guard over the Chapel and Modern Officer and Aircrew Selection Centre where once stood the old Triple Bay Hangar. On the corner of the Station Headquarters where the flag proudly flies, one of the few scars remain, part of the Gable Ended Hangar wall. If one looks closely around the airfield, a few Air Raid Shelters and Dispersal Pens can also be found.

Although becoming non-operational in 1958, but retaining its function as an Officer and Aircrew Selection Centre, the arrival of the Flying Clubs from Croydon in 1959 infused a new lease of life into Biggin Hill. It has survived to become one of the busiest civil airports in the country for light aircraft.

Original German aerial shot of Detling taken 1939

Chapter Four
DETLING
Robin J. Brooks

The Detling story dates back to 1915 when, with the expansion of the Royal Flying Corps and the Royal Naval Air Service, areas of land were being surveyed with a view to future use for flying. Detling was one of those surveyed, and later selected by the Director of Works. In June 1915 a small unit of 4 Curtiss aeroplanes, whose concern was the defence of London, arrived at the new airfield. Levelling and clearance of the ground was still under way as it had not been used for many years, even for agricultural purposes.

In 1916 the unit at Detling was enlarged and re-equipped with the Sopwith 1½ Strutter. The title of the unit was changed, and it became No. 3 Aeroplane Wing. In May 1916 the wing moved to Manston, and the following telegram was sent to the Air Department — "Admiralty: — Detling Air Station reduced to care and maintenance this day on units transfer to Manston." The move was in preparation for departing to France. On 14th October 1916 No. 3 Wing proceeded to Luxeuil.

The care and maintenance staff at Detling, plus three rather old naval aircraft, were the sole inhabitants until on 3rd April 1917, the airfield was transferred from the Naval Air Service to the Royal Flying Corps. From this time on units of the Corps used the field, but they did not stay long. On 1st April 1918 the Royal Naval Air Service and the Royal Flying Corps combined to form the nucleus of the Royal Air Force. Home defence fighters were based at Detling until 1919 when it was again reduced to care and maintenance.

In 1938, with the threat of another war, the Royal Auxiliary Air Force Squadrons began to build up strength. In August 1938, with the rapid expansion of the Royal Air Force, No. 500 (County of Kent) Squadron arrived at Detling, from Manston. The squadron of weekend pilots had just received the honour of being the first auxiliary squadron to be given a number. Now they were to be conscripted on a permanent basis.

Five Hundred Squadron were equipped with the Avro Anson Mk. 1. Carrying a crew of 3 to 4, the Anson then formed the backbone of the newly formed Coastal Command. A station headquarters was set up at Detling and the station opened as a Coastal Command airfield attached to No. 16 Group. The squadron were soon employed in reaching operational status ready for the inevitable war.

During the first month of operations, 500 Squadron flew 506 hours of convoy escorts from Detling. The main task of the squadron at this time was reconnaissance operations over the Channel and in the Dover Straits, together with convoy escorts through the Straits. The aircraft had adopted a very warlike appearance. The fuselages were camouflaged to blend in with the sea and, in addition to a bombload, two additional machine guns were added, firing through the side window. The Commanding Officer, Squadron Leader LeMay, had a 22mm cannon fitted to his Anson, which fired through the bottom of the fuselage. Tilling Stevens, of Maidstone, manufactured the gun mountings after an attempt by an Officer of the squadron to design and perfect a block and pin mounting, had proved a little precarious. The aircraft were called 'bristling porcupines' and had a very aggressive look about them.

On the 6th May 1939, 500 Squadron marched through Maidstone to receive the freedom of the town and to mark the squadron's affiliation with the county town. The Mayor of Maidstone took the salute, and the local population showed their appreciation and support for the Royal Air Force.

Empire Air Day at Detling was held on the 20th May 1939. Fifteen thousand people came to see what many felt was to be the last air show to be held in peacetime. The Ansons of 500 Squadron in their new camouflage thrilled the crowd with their display.

War was declared on September 3rd 1939 and immediately Detling was brought to a war status. The Germans began to attack our convoys in the Channel and, in retaliation, Coastal Command began to bomb enemy harbours. The squadron became a front line unit in this respect for, on the 5th September, an Anson of the squadron made the first RAF attack of the war when it bombed a U-boat caught on the surface. The incident helped boost the morale of the Anson crews because, in operational value the aircraft was basically obsolete. This, combined with other factors, resulted in many crashed and written-off aircraft.

On the 9th September 1939, Anson N5052 was on a sortie from Detling when it developed engine failure and was abandoned to crash near Canterbury, the crew safely baling out. The same day another Anson crashed into the sea off Whitstable. Another aircraft also suffered engine failure on approach to Detling and the crew abandoned it over Benenden. Flying Officer D. G. Mabey was the sole survivor from N5233, the rest of the crew were killed by the parachute fall.

Early in 1940 the 'phoney war' of 1939 began to change into real war. On the 1st January 1940 a flight of Ansons from 500 Squadron were attacked by nine Messerschmitt 109 fighters whilst on patrol over the Channel. They distinguished themselves by shooting down two of the fighters with the extra guns that were installed in the fuselage.

On the 25th May 1940 the Dunkirk evacuation began from France, and there arrived at Detling an amazing collection of long-forgotten aircraft. Pilot Officer D. H. Clarke reported for duty on 30th May flying a target-towing Blackburn Skua of No. 2 Anti-aircraft Co-operation unit stationed at Gosport. His orders were to patrol each night West of Dunkirk, dropping powerful flares to light up any attempt by the German Navy to interfere with the evacuation. Pilot Officer Clarke had precisely two hours night-flying experience.

The next morning, as his operation was not timed until after nightfall, he assisted the ground crews who were working on about fifty Fleet Air Arm

Ansons of 500 Squadron over Dover Harbour — 1938. Stationed at Detling (Kent Messenger)

Swordfish aircraft. These were due to take off on a figher patrol across the Dunkirk beaches. The idea was that the Germans would think the Swordfish to be the equally obsolescent Gladiator fighter, and would be frightened off by them. Unfortunately the Germans were far wiser.

Pilot Officer Clarke noticed some Blenheims which never left the ground. When he enquired why he was told "gas — they're fitted with tanks for spraying gas. Just in case the Jerries start using it."

The second fighter patrol of the morning was flown by Fleet Air Arm dive bombers and two-seater fighters. The patrol comprised thirty seven Blackburn Skuas and Blackburn Rocs. Pilot Officer Clarke watched the return of the patrol just before lunch-time. He recalled: "There were not many — I counted six. Where were the others? One belly flopped and I went across to see what had happened. The aircraft was a complete write-off. Bullets and cannon shells had ripped the fuselage from end to end, the after cockpit was sprayed liberally with blood. The front cockpit was worse. Two bullet holes through the back of the pilot's seat showed where he had been hit and his parachute, still in position, was saturated in blood. The instrument panel was shattered and on the floor was the remains of a foot." Of the original thirty seven aircraft, nine came back and five were written off after inspection. The remaining four aircraft were airborne within the hour. Clarke remarked: "They looked very pathetic limping back to Dunkirk, all alone."

On the night of 30th/31st May 1940, an incident that occurred at Detling placed the field firmly in the annals of World War Two. The Ansons had taken off on a mission over the enemy coast and were expected back soon after midnight. One of the Ansons, failing to release its bomb load, turned back for Detling. Crossing the Channel it developed engine failure. Worse was still to come for, when the aircraft came to line-up for the runway, the failed engine burst into flames. Approaching the outskirts of the airfield it began to lose height rapidly and a crash seemed inevitable. It landed heavily and slid across the field, the flames spreading along the fuselage. The bombs did not explode on impact but the fire must surely ignite them.

To Corporal Daphne Pearson, lying on her bunk in the Womens Auxiliary Air Force quarters, it was not unusual to hear the Ansons splutter a bit when returning from a raid. On this particular night, however, she heard and saw something that was terrifying and ominous. The Anson was burning, and had crashed across the airfield. The Medical Sections Corporal quickly pulled on her clothes and Wellington boots, seized her tin hat and ran out of the building toward the aircraft.

A dull glow identified it as she scrambled over a hedge, fell down an incline, over a slight bank until nearly at the burning wreckage, she saw two men staggering with a third between them. The third man, obviously in great pain, was screaming.

"He's got a broken back" one of the men gasped. "All right," she said, "leave him to me." In a daze the men made their way to the sick bay.

As Corporal Pearson began to attend to the injured pilot, he murmured about the fuel tanks and bombs aboard the plane. She then realized that at any moment the Anson would explode. Dragging the pilot over the ridge she put herself on top of him to protect him. He murmured something about his face and she saw that it had a lot of blood on it and a tooth was protruding from his upper jaw. In her own words:— "I reassured him about his face, and pulled the tooth out. Then the plane went up with a tremendous explosion."

They were only about thirty yards away from the blast. But for the ridge protecting them both from the splinters and the shock wave, they would have perished. So great was the blast that other helpers rushing to the scene were all blown flat onto the ground.

The ambulance arrived for the pilot, but only when she was satisfied that no-one else remained in the Anson did Daphne Pearson leave the scene where other bombs might explode at any minute. This total act was done entirely without thought for her own safety.

She received her commission in June, and the following month the 'London Gazette' announced that Corporal (now Assistant Section Officer) Pearson had been awarded the Empire Gallantry Medal. In August she went to the investiture at Buckingham Palace, and again in November 1941 to receive the George Cross in exchange for the Gallantry Medal. This very brave woman, though dogged all her life by ill health, went on to serve Detling and the Royal Air Force until the end of the war.

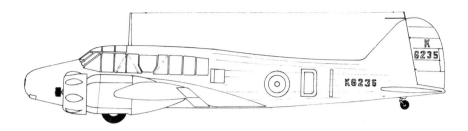

Avro 652 Anson Mk.1 500 Squadron Royal Air Force. Detling 1939

The months at Detling ran into August, and the Battle of Britain was reaching its zenith. Detling was still home to a large and varied selection of aircraft. No. 801 Squadron, Fleet Air Arm, flying Skuas and Rocs again were engaged on bombing enemy gun sites at Cap Blanc Nez. No. 253 and 254 Squadrons flying Bristol Blenheims were also based at Detling.

The Ansons of 500 Squadron flew 1,386 hours during the month of May, again with many losses. There were some victories however. On 18th July 1940, one of the Ansons shot down a Messerschmitt 110 with 500 rounds of ammunition, no mean task for an aircraft as slow as the Anson.

With August the Luftwaffe raids on British soil increased. As Adolf Hitler's 'Eagle Day' dawned, Tuesday 13th August, Detling became the target for a raid.

The station had been relatively quiet all day until at 1600 hours eighty six Junkers 87 (Stuka) dive-bombers of Hauptmann Von Brauchitschs Luftflotte 2 appeared out of the cloud, approaching the airfield. It was a dire raid. Shrieking from thick cloud cover, the Stukas achieved the measure of surprise they needed. Many of the airmen and airwomen on the field were taking tea in the mess when the first bombs fell. The marksmanship of the German airmen was good. Every runway was devastated, the entire length of each was just bomb craters, rock and earth. Fire started in every hangar, eventually to spread, rendering twenty two aircraft destroyed. As the Operations Room disappeared in one large explosion, the Station Commander Group Captain Edward Davis, a former tennis champion, fell dead with a piece of concrete driving straight through his skull.

Stationed at Detling at this time were many Maidstone people. These were members of the Detling permanent staff, and members of 500 Squadron. One permanent Non Commissioned Officer was a Mr Foster of Bearsted. Then a Corporal, his trade was in the Medical section at Detling. He recalls the raid that day:— "I arrived at Detling in June 1940. I had been evacuated from Dunkirk because I was with the Air Force in France before Jerry marched in. We came up on the train from Dover to Paddock Wood where the 'soup kitchens' were set up for the men returning from Dunkirk. After Uxbridge and Kirton-Lindsey I came to Detling. About that raid, — I remember about four o' clock someone mentioned that many German aircraft had got through and were approaching the airfield. Sure enough, minutes after all hell was let loose. The sick bay was not directly hit but many fragments and rubble from the Operations room which was quite close fell on the roof. I know many of the Army men manning the Bofors guns for airfield defence were killed. I was kept very busy that night, many of the injuries were very bad, plus of course the dead. When it was all over, there were a lot of burning buildings. After this raid the Ministry dediced to disperse much of the camp around the surrounding area. We moved the sick bay to a house called 'Woodlands'. Nizzen huts were put up in the garden to make more room. The WAAFs went to a stone mansion somewhere towards Sittingbourne. Shortly after this raid, I think the end of August, Detling received another one but because many of us were not actually on the camp it was not so bad. I left Detling in April 1941 so I saw many of the bad times there."

Mr P. Dunlop of Hawkhurst was in the Operations room when it received a direct hit. He recalls:

"On that afternoon there were about ten of us in the Operations room which formed one side of a hollow square — this was the form in which the then recently completed Operations block was constructed. The roof was double skinned reinforced concrete — each skin about twelve inches thick — and between the skins there was a layer of dry ballast four feet thick.

"I can recall the Commanding Officer taking a call on the direct line from the Observer Corps. He turned round to everyone and said it looks as though a bunch of JU 87's has got through and are coming this way. Sure enough a couple of minutes later the raid started and the Operations room was hit twice — once on the North West corner and again smack in the middle. To the best of my recollection only three of us survived — the rest were buried in ballast. The survivors just happened to be lucky enough to be standing in the only corner of the room which the vast cone of ballast, which poured from the fractured roof, failed to reach."

In 1940 Mr Dunlop was a Leading Aircraftman No. 812293.

Again from the diary of Mr. W. Yates of Maidstone, a very vivid account of the ordeal of 500 Squadron during the raid:—

"13th August 1940. The B Flight night-duty groundcrew of 500 (County of Kent) Squadron finished their evening meal, and waited in and around the Dennis lorry which would take them to the Anson aircraft parked in fields alongside the Yelsted road at the north-east corner of Detling aerodrome.

"Faintly, in the distance, Maidstone's air-raid sirens were heard, and then the drone of aircraft. These aircraft could be seen approaching the airfield from about 2 miles away to the south-east at a height of about 5,000 feet. The formation was much larger than had been seen in the area before — so much so that it prompted one of the squadron armourers, Bill Yates, to announce that he "didn't know we had so many". This remark almost qualified for "Famous last words" as Yates clambered to the Dennis' canvas top, and began a count of the aircraft. He had passed the 30 mark when the leading machine dipped its port wing in a diving turn, and became without any shadow of doubt — a Stuka. (The 'Luftwaffe War Diaries' say that 86 of these Ju 87 dive-bombers reached Detling.)

"Realisation of what was about to happen had now dawned on everybody, and caused a concerted dash for the nearest shelter. The 'commentator' on the Dennis, began his sprint during the 10 foot jump from the lorry's roof, and found himself beside Bill Harris, another B Flight armourer. After the first few yards a dull thud came from behind, but this was not the first of the bombs arriving — a backward glance showed that it was 'Binder' Hammond (a third armourer) who had tripped over a kerb, and hammered himself onto a concrete road. The same glance revealed bombs now falling from Stukas, and a hangar was seen to take at least 2 direct hits before disappearing in smoke and flames.

"Other bombs were now catching up with the armourers, and dust and debris almost obliterated their vision, but apart from receiving odd thumps from clods of earth or whatever, both were undamaged when they reached the comparative safety of a shelter. Inside, the noise was still very much in evidence, earth was falling from the roof and walls, and both men were surprised to find that, during their dash, their mouths had filled with dirt. The shelter already held a number of airmen and W.A.A.F.s who were quietly waiting for whatever was to come next.

"In fact, the din subsided, the shelter steadied, all became quiet, and the raid, having lasted 7 long minutes, was over. But nobody was prepared for the havoc around them as they left the shelter. The orderly lines of billets, the newly-painted cookhouse, and the neat concrete roads were no longer there. The camp had been destroyed — it was now a rubbish dump in a ploughed field, and for these 'week-end airmen' of the Auxiliary Air Force who had been part of this camp since it was opened for them as a brand-new aerodrome back in October 1938, feelings were very mixed — a stunned numbness at the obvious heavy loss of life, and hot anger at what had been done to R.A.F. Detling.

"Finding that sufficient help was available for the work of rescue, first-aid for the wounded, and recovery of bodies from debris, Harris and Yates made for the squadron armoury which was battered but recognisable. Here they found a note telling them that the bombed hangar contained an Anson which, before the raid, had been taken inside with bombs still aboard — and would the duty armourers get them off.

"The 'duty armourers' started for the hangar, but when about to enter it were confronted by Cpl. Dockery (Bomb Disposal) who told Harris to " ——— off, and take your mate with you!" The corporal then continued to plant his little red flags by the sides of holes at the bottoms of which were unexploded

Detling Aerodrome 1979

(Len Pilkington)

bombs. Despite this discouragement, the Anson's bombs were removed — not from bravado but because of a healthy respect for the reactions of Flt. Sgt. 'Pincher' Martin should he discover that the request in his note had not been complied with. The 2 bombs were carried from the remains of the hangar, and left for Cpl. Dockery to dispose of, but with hindsight it was difficult to see why anyone had bothered, since the aircraft and the hangar had already been wrecked.

"Shortly afterwards, roll-calls were held in order to establish casualty lists — one subsequent report puts the number killed at 66, whilst another gives 97. The two armourers were now free to organise a 'brew-up' in the cottage serving as an armoury on the Yelsted road, and whilst enjoying their first cuppa, Harris drew attention to the fact that Yates was now "shaking like a leaf", and the latter had to point out that the former appeared to be in the same sorry state. In fact it can be supposed that everybody was shaken, but 500 Squadron was nevertheless operating its aircraft again in less than 24 hours.

"The day groundcrew who were being relieved, undertook to call on relatives of survivors who lived locally, and to let them have the news which they had doubtless been anxiously awaiting — the raid had been clearly seen and heard from parts of Maidstone. Notification of casualties was left to official sources. Virtually all camp facilities having been destroyed — sleeping quarters included — a number of additional cottages in the Yelsted Road were requisitioned, and these housed B Flight groundcrews until March 1941 when 500 Squadron started a move to Bircham Newton in Norfolk."

Some of the officers of 'B' flight had a premonition about the raid. On the day previously Squadron Leader Douglas Pain had walked from the mess anteroom and had heard the unmistakeable noise of enemy aircraft engines. Looking eastwards he noticed a 'chain' of aircraft circling the dummy airfield at Lenham. These were Stukas going into line astern in a half circle. They made one or two complete circuits at a height of about 10,000 feet then, to his amazement, suddenly made off towards the coast. He assumed that they had been frightened off by having no cloud cover on this particular afternoon, but it stuck in Douglas Pain's mind that it might just be a rehearsal for the next day.

On the fateful day, he was actually returning from an anti-submarine patrol and had to land on the airfield which was full of craters. His story of seeing the 'home' field in such a mess is worthy of print.

"We took off on patrol at about 06.30 hours on the 13th and set course for the North Foreland, our usual sea departure point. The crew were: myself as pilot, Flying Officer Bob Jay as Navigator, Pilot Officer George Bliss, air gunner and Sergeant Oakwell, wireless operator. There were cotton-wool balls of cumulus cloud forming at about 3,000 ft. in a bright sky.

"The old 'Anson' bumbled along. I said over the intercom, with what turned out to be remarkable prescience, "Detling is going to catch a packet today." No one else spoke!

"Our convoy patrol from Detling was uneventful. We landed at Bircham Newton in Norfolk to refuel before returning to our home base, just in time for lunch. The weather was glorious and after lunch we lingered in the anteroom over a glass of port. Bircham Newton was famous for its food and drink.

"We took off and flew back down the coast. Whilst over the Thames Estuary we found a wrecked ship and decided to have some front gun practice on it. I had shot down a Heinkel 111H with my front gun on the previous June 12th, so we regarded ourselves as rather superior to Hurricanes, if not quite up to the standard of Spitfires!

"As we approached Detling the sky clouded over, 10/10ths. at 3,000 ft. There also seemed to be something strange about the airfield. Scars of yellow earth all over the surface. Then the hangars — good God! They looked rather like badly damaged kitchen colanders. It was unbelievable that this could really happen to our home."

"We sailed slowly round the circuit, noting the damage. The operations room had obviously taken a 1200 pounder bomb right in the centre. All the messes had been blown to bits except the WAAF's dining room. We landed carefully, picking our way through the craters that covered the airfield, and taxied back to 'A' flight hangars and offices, which were more or less in one piece. We had missed the whole show because of our dallying on our return. How lucky can you be.

"We leaped out of the aircraft and made for the remains of the operations room. The rescue work was in full swing but aircrew were not encouraged to take part in this sort of thing and we were sent back to our various messes to sort ourselves out as best we could. A 1200 pounder had landed in the middle of our anteroom, but on the edge of the crater stood our radiogram, quite undamaged and still playable. I remember that my beer tankard was the only one which was completely undamaged amongst all the men's silver tankards.

"Later on we were able to hear of various people's experiences. I remember three stories in particular, all three of a very light hearted nature. One concerned Peter Duff-Mitchell of 'A' flight, 500 Squadron. He was in the bath having recently landed from an operational sortie when he heard a loud noise of engines overhead. He jumped out of the bath and squinted out of the top of the frosted glass window ... He saw what he thought were Spitfires and was surprised when they all started diving on the airfield. Suddenly the ghastly truth dawned on him and he took off for the air raid shelter, stark naked and waving a large bath towel. Luckily he made it — in company with numbers of WAAF's! This must have been the original case of 'streaking'!

"Our squadron commander, Wing Commander C. H. Turner was making a simulated blind approach under the 'hood' in one of 'B' flight's Ansons with Squadron Leader Pat Green sitting beside him as safety pilot. The 'Hood' was a device for aircrew to use to practise the art of blind flying. Suddenly the whole airfield seemed to erupt in their faces. Pat Green whipped the hood from the eyes of the astonished 'Winco' who was presented with the sight of his squadron being reduced to produce. They opened the engines flat out and flying low, hastily landed at Rochester airfield a few miles to the north west.

"The third amusing incident concerned Flying Officer Harold Jones, our excellent gunnery leader. He was doing an inspection of an Anson in 'A' flight hangar with one of his airmen. Suddenly bombs started to fall all around them. He said afterwards: 'You know, it was very strange. There were only two of us and one Anson in that hangar, yet we kept running head on into each other.' I think this gives a good idea of the sort of thing induced by a sudden and unexpected blitz."

Though part of 500 Squadron, 'A' flight was situated across the road from the main airfield by the side of Thurnham Lane. The Ansons of the flight being dispersed among the trees and shrubs in the field. Flight Sergeant J. C. Thompson, a Maidstone man, takes up the story from the opposite side of the airfield.

"Tucked away in the woods behind our dispersal was a large house. It is still there today, but exposed now to view from the main Maidstone road because the thick copse has been removed. The lady who lived there used to provide us with cups of tea or bottles of lemonade and the occasional sandwich or home-made cake at a very reasonable cost. We would slink off, one or two at a time as we were always hungry. Providing the work load did not suffer, the powers that be used to turn a blind eye. It so happened that in the afternoon of the 13th I was sitting in this house regaling myself with a cup of tea and a wad. The lady's small son came to me and tugged at my knee, with his sad and solemn little face turned up to me. He tried to get me to go outside but at first I was reluctant as these few moments respite from work were all too few. Then, faced with my inaction he said "Mister! They ain't our'n!"

"Brushing a few crumbs from my lap I rose and went outside with him. Calm and confident in all the authority invested in my corporal's stripes and war experience, I murmured inane phrases of reassurance and encouragement. We walked out to a small clearing, hand in hand, and I directed my gaze upwards.

"My attention at first was drawn to a small cluster of single engined fighters, circling high slightly to the North East. I felt sure these were Hurricanes, and told the lad so. There was no gunfire and nothing to cause any undue apprehension. Then I looked over the top of the trees towards the unseen airfield. Roughly to the South West and above the airfield, a string of large aircraft circling, were peeling off into near vertical dives. One glance at the pronounced flat 'W' of their wings was enough for even my poor experience, even before the first sounds of that wailing scream could be head.

"All I could think of at first was the small gunpit, armed with a Lewis gun, sited in our dispersal field. Hurriedly I told the boy to go back and hide with his Mum in their cellar, without even knowing if they possessed such an amenity. I ran as fast as I could out to the edge of the wood and frequent thumps could be felt through one's feet. When I reached the edge of the wood, I was amazed to see the gunpit deserted and the gun still shrouded in the green canvas cover. At the far end of the field, an Anson was engaged in a compass swing with both engines ticking over. I saw the crews running in a crouched position towards a shelter near our nissen hut.

"Discretion being the better part of valour, I beat a strategic retreat back to the edge of the wood. Looking towards the main camp, I could see the Stukas hard at work, and to my amazement I saw what appeared to be the complete assembled roof of one of the corrugated iron hangars rise lazily high into the air where it seemed to hover for several minutes before it wobbled and came crashing down.

"The whole terrifying business seemed to be going on for hours but probably only lasted for about a quarter of an hour. I remember being very disappointed that none of our own fighters put in an appearance. When comparative calm once more reigned, I started to run towards our nissen hut hoping to meet up with some people and do something about the Anson still running its engines. By now columns of smoke and occasional explosions were coming from all around the area.

"As I ran along near the edge of the wood, a giant gentle hand snatched me up off my feet and seemed to be holding me suspended on a very comfortable bubble of air. I remember thinking how pleasant the sensation was and how quiet and peaceful. Suddenly the giant hand seemed to change its mind. Without warning I was forcibly plunged into the thick thorny bushes, gasping for breath. It was a very painful experience, both going in to the bush and coming out. Obviously it must have been the blast from one of the exploding bombs."

The raid was seen approaching from the many fields and houses that were in the vicinity of the airfield. Mrs Jean Johnson then lived at Linton with her parents and saw the German planes cover the sky. In her words, "the planes just dived on Detling". Mrs Johnson was employed at a bank in Sittingbourne. On the afternoon of the raid, the homeward journey took much longer. The Sittingbourne/Maidstone bus crossed Detling airfield but on this particular afternoon it ended the journey at the 'Three Squirrels' public house. The travelling public had to walk along the road heading to Cold Blow Lane and eventually out to Detling village.

"This was the pattern for about a week after the big raid, nothing was allowed to pass through Detling airfield," said Mrs Johnson.

Of the number of WAAF's stationed at the airfield at this time, one was to endure the raid and to die tragically later in an air crash whilst still in the service. She did however write to her close friend Ann Griffiths of Offham, who was also in the WAAF's at the same time though posted from Detling before the raid. An extract from her letter portrays the terror that she felt.

"I expect you heard of the awful raid of the 13th August. I was just leaving the Ops block and posting a letter, then suddenly out of a cloudy sky they swooped. There were about fifty or sixty Huns and they let hell loose. Never

80

have I heard such a noise. I ran like fury with two airmen, they poor dears got killed by bullets in the back as we were machine-gunned as we ran. I have never in my whole life been so utterly terrified. I got hit by some flying wood so I threw myself on the ground while everything blew up as they dive-bombed.

"All of B flight went up including planes just by me. Afterwards I got cracking and cleared the road by the sick bay with my hands so that the ambulances could pass.

"After that raid it has been continual, in fact we spent night and day underground and work went to blazes. Fortunately only one WAAF was seriously hurt.

"At last every-one has moved off camp and it is only used for flying, a damn good job! We are all billeted out, which is fine and we work 'somewhere in England'. The poor old WAAF quarters got somewhat bashed about, our new messing hut caught a packet and every window was smashed. I worked for forty eight hours after the main raid without sleep and carried on with very little for three weeks and then got three weeks' leave."

For many of the young girls, the majority of them from Kent, the war was beginning to have an effect on them. Most of the WAAF's at Detling at this time had not experienced the noise, confusion and death that the enemy were now dealing out.

In spite of the hit on the Operations room and the casualties, the Airwomen went on plotting the enemy's course in another building. Corporal Robins, a Non Commissioned Officer, was awarded the Military Medal for her courage under fire. She was in a dug-out by the Operations room when it received the fatal hit. A number of men were killed and two seriously wounded in the same dug-out. Though dust, fumes and rubble filled the shelter, Corporal Robins immediately went to the assistance of the wounded and rendered first aid. She fetched a stretcher and stayed with the wounded until they were evacuated. The citation on 20th December 1940 stated that she displayed courage and coolness of a very high order in a position of extreme danger.

Another Military Medal was awarded to Sergeant Youle of the WAAF as a result of her courage during this same attack. She was on duty in the station telephone exchange when it received a direct hit with other bombs in close proximity. Her staff were subjected to a rain of debris and splinters and to the noise of exploding bombs. It was solely due to the cool bravery and the superb example set by Sergeant Youle that the telephone operators carried on their task with calmness and complete efficiency at a most dangerous time for all. It is praise indeed for all of the Women's section to say that the Operations room and all essential services were back in operation the next morning.

The various taxiways and dispersal points around the perimeter of the airfield were badly bombed as well as the main runways and administration buildings. One machine gun post and two anti-aircraft sites were direct hits killing all the Army personnel manning them. One Gunner situated in a similar post was heard to say that he had preferred it at Dunkirk!

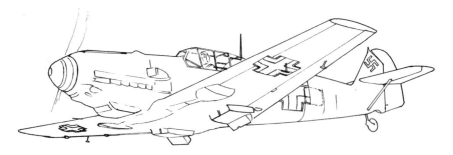

Me.109E

As the Stukas spread devastation and death at Detling, the local population of Maidstone were gearing themselves to lend aid and assistance to the stricken area. Casualty Clearing Officer Wallace Beale, a Maidstone undertaker, sped to the shattered airfield together with the local units of the Civil Defence. The scene that they found would have made many a weaker man ill. Of the sixty-seven people killed, many needed only five foot coffins reserved for unidentified remains. A further ninety-four were injured and many of them could not be treated in the station sick bay.

Detling was a mess! The complete surprise of the attack had shocked all of the service and the civilian people of the airfield and the surrounding area.

A second raid on Detling took place on 31st August. The main German bomber force was making to the Coastal Command airfield at Eastchurch. When over the coast of Britain the force divided and the fighter escort turned for Detling. Captain Eschwege, the German escort commander leading 1/3G 52 comprising Messerschmitt 109's and 110's swept low over the boundary at Detling firing cannon and machine guns. Again the raid took the airfield by surprise. The petrol and oil dumps were set on fire creating a black smoke cloud that hung above the airfield for hours. The main electricity supply cable was cut by the attack and the airfield was totally out of use for fifteen hours with no communications whatever. The main approach roads to the field were blocked by rubble from the blasts. This time only a few casualties were reported but the devastation was again immense.

During the following night, whilst clearance from the previous raid was still going on, Detling was attacked by several lone raiders. It did not say much for the German High Command Intelligence Service for, whilst Detling was an important airfield, it was not a sector field for Fighter Command.

Detling was now getting the reputation among service personnel that a posting to this airfield meant sleepless nights and much bombing and devastation from the enemy. Being six hundred feet above sea level, no amount of artificial camouflage could properly conceal the true identity of the airfield, not even the occasional hill fog.

82

On the 2nd September 1940 the Luftwaffe carried out a high level attack on the station. A Gruppe of Dornier 17's dropped about one hundred high explosive bombs causing great damage. Again the cloud afforded the Luftwaffe good cover and the element of surprise was kept. Only when the first bombs began to fall did the airfield siren give warning to the surrounding district. The airfield was rendered unserviceable for three hours. The services of the Civil Defence and the local population were again needed to put the airfield back into action.

This was the last sizeable raid on Detling. Sometime later in the month, Adolf Hitler changed the German bombing policy. Having failed to eliminate the Royal Air Force and the airfields, he turned his attention to the bigger cities. Whilst it was bad for the civilian population it was a breath of air for Lord Dowding, the chief of Fighter Command.

1940 passed into 1941. Christmas that year was wet with thick mist and low cloud. This grounded the Luftwaffe as well as the squadrons at Detling allowing the festive period to pass peacefully.

In the new year, 500 Squadron were still carrying the war over enemy territory. A new squadron had arrived at Detling. This was an anti-aircraft co-operative squadron used expressly for target towing to enable the anti-aircraft guns target practice and range finding. Again it consisted of a variety of long obsolete aircraft, Hawker Hectors, Gloster Gladiators, Fairey Battles and Blenheims.

On the administrative side of the airfield, the builders finished renewing much that the Luftwaffe had knocked down. The WAAF's, having been dispersed out to the surrounding houses since the big raid, were now back at Detling, in brick or wooden billets. Many were evacuated under canvas after the raids. Each airwoman was issued with a ground sheet and about six blankets. Hooks were fastened to the tent poles, and uniforms hung up inside at night. In the morning, the WAAF Officers marched the girls back to Detling. This was the pattern for some considerable time, so great jubilation was felt by all when they were allowed to move back into permanent accommodation.

On the 7th April 1941, 500 Squadron changed their Ansons for the Bristol Blenheim and shortly after received the American Lockheed Hudson. This also ended an era for the squadron as they were posted to Bircham Newton in Norfolk. Since 1938, Detling and 500 Squadron had been synonymous with each other.

In June 1941, No. 248 Squadron arrived, bringing the sound of the Bristol Beaufighter to the district. By now the tide of war was running in favour of the allies. Our aircraft began to roam freely across occupied Europe.

In April 1942 members of No. 2768 Squadron of the Royal Air Force Regiment, stationed at Detling, were to take a period of guarding Buckingham Palace. This was the first time the Regiment had ever had the honour. At the same time the Archbishop of Canterbury dedicated the new station Chapel at Detling, the old one having been badly hit in the first raid.

Detling now entered a new phase. The airfield was transferred from Coastal Command to Fighter Command (General Ops). New squadrons came for rigorous

Detling 1979 — 'T 2' Type Hangar   (Robin J. Brooks)

Detling 1979 — Pillbox around perimeter   (Robin J. Brooks)

Detling 1979 — Entrance to shelters and airfield perimeter   (Robin J. Brooks)

fighter training for brief periods. No. 318 (Polish squadron) and No. 602 (County of Glasgow) squadrons were just two that passed through the station.

In November 1943, No. 603 Squadron Royal Auxiliary Air Force arrived at Detling with Spitfires. Their operations included many offensive and intruder sweeps into enemy territory. Flying with the squadron at this time was Flight Sergeant Pierre Closterman, a Frenchman who was to make a name for himself both in the Air Force and as an author after the war. With a change in flying policy, several squadrons were now flying together forming large wings of aircraft. The Detling wing was commanded by Wing Commander Mike Crossley DSO, DFC and comprised Nos. 80, 229 and 274 Squadrons. These large formations of Spitfires roamed across occupied Europe as well as escorting the very large bomber formations that were now hitting the heart of Germany.

On the 6th June 1944, D. Day, the wing gave support to the allied invasion. No. 567 Squadron also arrived at Detling with a mixture of aircraft consisting of Oxfords, Barracudas, Hurricanes and Martinets. No. 602 Squadron were posted to Airfield 125, one of the many Advanced Landing Grounds created to support the invasion.

With the war in Europe drawing to a close, rapid changes in squadrons operating from Detling were taking place. No. 504 Squadron came to support the Arnhem landings with their Spitfires, and then left. Gradually the station was run down in operational value and on January 1st 1945 it was placed in a care and maintenance state, the third time in its career.

This was rather a premature end for such an active airfield but being still just a grass airfield and with aircraft becoming heavier and more sophisticated it did not warrant the expenditure necessary to bring it to 1945 standard. It did not sink entirely into obscurity. Sometime after the end of the war, No. 615 Gliding School arrived to give instruction to the cadets of the newly formed Air Training Corps. When this unit moved to Royal Air Force Kenley, the civil gliders of the Kent Gliding Club took over the field. With the departure of this club to more permanent premises at Challock airfield, Detling settled back into peace and tranquility. The land was returned back to the owners and the Kent County Council acquired some of the land for the annual Kent County Show.

Today the indications that the open stretch of green land was once a very active airfield are few to the eye. One hangar and some crew-rooms still stand, now used by local industry. Several underground shelters and some of the hard perimeter track are to be seen and the original radio tower still stands, now in use with Pye for radio communication. The action is written in the combat reports and memories of the airmen and women who flew and served at Detling during its war career.

Many of the serving people settled in the locality at the end of the war. Trying to trace some of the heroes of Detling is a little more difficult.

Daphne Pearson served at several Bomber Command stations until the end of her service career. As a civilian she set to work 'job hunting'. She applied for forty six posts and for forty six times it came to nothing. Finally she joined the

Detling 1979. The original Airfield Billets   (Robin J. Brooks)

Civil Service and reached Assistant Governor in the Prison Service. Then her health again failed her, and she spent many years undergoing treatment in and out of hospital.

Today she resides in Australia and has taken to writing. Her connections with Kent and Detling are very strong. The years spent before she enlisted in the Woman's Auxiliary Air Force were spent as manageress of the Ditton Court Farm shop near Maidstone. Her home was in one of the houses almost opposite the shop, which is today still in business though it has grown since Miss Pearson's time.

Of the many other men and women who saw distinguished service at Detling, they are scattered about England and the World at large. Many have since died, some from the injuries that they received from the war, some from injuries received at Detling during those dark days. Time has erased some of the horrors from many memories, others have scars to remind them of the past.

Detling today is at rest, sheep graze on the grass that once was churned up with aircraft and bombs. It is a fitting tribute that sitting in the centre of the airfield is a navigational aid of the Civil Air Traffic Control system, guiding and helping the many civil aircraft that now fly overhead in this time of peace.

Chapter Five

MANSTON – FRONT LINE AIRFIELD

By David G. Collyer

The start of July 1940 at Manston was relatively quiet after the hectic days of the previous two months. During the Dunkirk evacuation various squadrons had been based at Manston and had operated from there to cover the beaches.

Squadron Leader William L. Grout was serving on the station as a Senior NCO on the Station H.Q. staff. He recalls the situation as follows:

"At the time of Dunkirk we had no idea that there was anything going on, and we were not told anything. However, we suspected that something was 'in the wind' when assorted aircraft started landing at Manston. One of these was a Westland Lysander flown, to everybody's surprise by a LAC Clerk, who made a satisfactory, if somewhat 'dodgy' landing. The only thing which we did know was that personnel visiting Ramsgate were instructed not to wear uniform. My future father-in-law was a Master Butcher in York Street, Ramsgate and lived next-door at No. 4a, the Old Police Station. I kept a change of clothes there, and was able to visit the harbour area. I saw crowds of dishevelled men in an assortment of clothes being landed, and thought them to be refugees. It was only later that we learned that the evacuation had taken place."

600 Squadron with their black-painted Blenheim night-fighters were stationed at the East Camp until 16th May, when 604 Squadron with their day-fighter Blenhiems relieved them. 151 Squadron was also at Manston with their Hawker Hurricanes, and 264 Squadron used the airfield while operating their Defiant fighters over Dunkirk. 600 Squadron returned on 19th June and Manston saw the tattered remnants of the squadrons sent to support the British Expeditionary Force stage through Manston on their return.

Mr Len Wallis remembers the preparations which had been made for the protection of personnel at the airfield:

"I was a Leading Aircraftman Storekeeper, later promoted to Corporal. I was posted to Manston in April 1938, after serving 5 years in Egypt. This was my second visit to Manston, having been posted there as a raw recruit in 1930. As a Corporal I did a number of duties which were normal in peacetime, but there were additional ones in war-time. I did guard duties at a little farm just outside the airfield, on the main Margate road, checking the identity of all persons and vehicles, including buses. (The No. 9 bus route from Margate to Minster ran right through the Camp.) In addition to preparing for aircraft, numerous air raid shelters were built of brick and wood (Mole Hills). They were alright for bomb blast, but a bomb dropping on or near the entrance

Manston
Flugplatz

Länge (ostw. Greenw.): 1° 21′   Nördl. Breite: 51° 21′
Zielhöhe über NN: 46 m

Maßstab: 1 : 17 500

1. 3 Flugzeughallen	etwa	6 740 qm	7.	Reinwasserbehälter
2. 6 Flugzeugboxen	etwa	2 250 qm	8.	Schießstand
3. Abstellplätze für Flugzeuge, mit			9.	Luftschutzanlagen
Splitterschutzwällen umgeben			10.	Peilanlage
4. Unterkunfts- und Nebengebäude	etwa	34 000 qm	11.	kleine Funkstation mit 2 Funkmasten etwa 25 m hoch
5. Munitionslager	etwa	2 250 qm	12.	Flakstellungen
6. Tankstellen für Flugzeuge			13.	Kleinkampfanlagen mit Rundumhindernissen
Bebaute Fläche	etwa	45 240 qm		

Gleisanschluß nicht vorhanden

Manston (13.7.42) Target Map   (Christopher R. Elliott)

88

caught the whole thing ablaze. At Manston there were underground tunnels which were there in 1930 when I first went to Manston, little did I know that 10 years later I would be sitting in those very tunnels, which ran the whole length of the Camp, sheltering from Jerry bombs."

Squadron Leader 'Bill' Grout recounts the build-up to the Battle of Britain at Manston:

"During the two months following the Dunkirk evacuation, things were relatively quiet, but spasmodic raids by the enemy continued on a small scale. However, the manning of the station was gradually reduced, and on 11th June the Commanding Officer (Wing Commander Hanmer) was posted and handed over to a previously retired officer. This officer was serving as a civilian Senior Administrative Officer, but who now donned uniform as Squadron Leader Osbourne, and assumed Command."

On 2nd July, Air Vice Marshal Keith Park, A.O.C. No. 11 Group visited Manston to present the D.S.M. to Sergeant Holmes of 600 Squadron, and No. 1 'M' Balloon Unit was sent to Manston to assist in the defences following the dropping of high explosive and incendiary bombs. How long the balloons remained is not certain:

"I didn't see any balloons flown over the airfield, the only ones I saw were flown over the Air Sea Rescue launch base at Ramsgate." ('Bill' Grout)

The first raids on Manston were of little consequence, but the airfield defences had been strengthened in May with the posting of Royal Artillery gunners and the London Irish Regiment to defend the airfield from attacks which were expected at any time. Royal Engineers were also attached to Manston for trench digging and the erection of barbed wire in the surrounding area.

Procedure in the event of an air raid alert was somewhat complicated:

"When a 'Yellow Alert' was issued, we all had to parade outside the station Headquarters. Airmen who were detailed for airfield defence were equipped with rifles and NCO's with pistols. We then waited for the 'Red Alert', when the defence personnel would take up their posts and the remainder would make their way to the shelter under the parade ground via the entrance out-side the Dining Hall. Often the 'Red Alert' came too late for the airmen to reach the shelters, and on one occasion while we were at the stand-to we heard the whistling of a bomb overhead. This fell on the bomb dump, but proved to be a dud and did not explode. During the height of the Battle of Britain 'Yellow Alerts' were issued so frequently that the above system was abandoned." ('Bill' Grout)

The Battle of Britain proper started with anti-shipping operations by the Luftwaffe, and squadrons of fighters from Hornchurch, Rochford and other No. 11 Group airfields, were sent to Manston to help protect the convoys. On 8th July 74 Squadron was operating from Manston when Pilot Officer Stevenson

Remains of Manston underground hangar, Allard Grange, constructed to house Handley-Page O/100 heavy bombers in 1917-18.
(via Geoff. Williams)

and Sergeant Mould attacked four Bf.109's over the airfield. One was shot down in flames, and Flight Lieutenant Measures and Pilot Officer Dowding attacked a Heinkel He.111 over the Channel and it crashed into the sea in flames. Pilot Officer Stevenson returned to Manston where he crashed in Spitfire P9465 which had been damaged in combat, joining the Spitfire of Pilot Officer McMullen of 54 Squadron which had force landed the previous day after being damaged in a similar encounter.

The pilots of 74 Squadron were up and about early the following day flying a dawn patrol at 03.45 hrs. Encountering a mixed bag of Dorniers and Messerschmitts over the Channel, they shot down two of the bombers and one fighter. Two other Bf.109's collided with each other during the engagement. At 10.30 hrs Red Section took off to climb steeply over Margate to join Yellow Section which was attacking a Dornier Do.17P reconnaissance bomber. The bomber, which was escorted by some thirty Bf.109's crashed at Boulogne, while four enemy fighters were downed, and another two damaged. Pilot Officer Cobden force landed his Spitfire P9399 at Manston, together with K9863 (Pilot Officer Freebourne) and that of Sergeant Mould, all pilots being uninjured. After this fine effort, A.V.M. Park called in at the airfield during the evening to congratulate the pilots of 74 Squadron.

From this time flights from squadrons based at Sector Stations (Biggin Hill, Hornchurch, etc) were dispatched to operate from airfields such as Manston, Hawkinge and Lympne, they being designated Forward Landing Grounds.

54 Squadron was also in action on 9th July, 'B' Flight encountering a silver painted Heinkel He.59 seaplane while on their fourth patrol of the day. This seaplane was escorted by twenty Bf.109's which were attacked off Deal at 19.30 hrs. Flight Lieutenant A.C. 'Al' Deere DFC, a New Zealand pilot of 54 Squadron, collided head-on with one of the enemy fighters. Although the engine stopped, the propeller blades being bent back horizontally, Fl Lt Deere managed to glide back to within five miles of Manston. He was badly bruised in the forced landing, but otherwise unhurt, his Spitfire P9398 'Kiwi' was declared a 'write-off'. At the same time another 54 Squadron pilot, Pilot Officer Gaston, was shot down near Manston and was killed. Pilot Officer 'Jonnie' Alan forced the He.59 to land near the Goodwin Sands and it was later towed in and beached at Walmer, the crew being interned. This seaplane was painted with Red Cross markings and carried the letters D-ASUO, but was believed to be carrying wireless equipment used to direct Luftwaffe aircraft to the convoys passing through the Dover Straits. At the end of the day, 54 Squadron had lost two pilots killed, the toll after ten days fighting being six killed and two pilots injured. The squadron was now reduced to twelve pilots and eight aircraft, thirteen aircraft having been lost or damaged during that period.

Fog in the Channel hampered the Luftwaffe convoy attacks on 12th July, but at 16.30 hrs Squadron Leader 'Sailor' Malan, together with Sergeant Mould and Pilot Officer Stevenson, led an attack on three Heinkel He.111's bombing a ship off Margate. The Spitfires of 74 Squadron shot down all three bombers, and the grateful sailors saluted the pilots as they flew over the vessel they had just saved.

Apart from routine patrols, all remained quiet until 19th July, when another early patrol by 74 Squadron saw them going to the aid of a Hurricane of 242 Squadron over Dover. 'Sailor' Malan shot down one of the attacking Bf.109's and Pilot Officer Stevenson got the other. The next day saw 65 Squadron operating from Manston to patrol the Medway, engaging enemy fighters and bombers. Another Heinkel He.59 ambulance seaplane was attacked, after it had been established that they were not 'bona fide' Red Cross aircraft.

While on patrol at 17.30 hrs on 24th July, two sections of 74 Squadron were vectored onto three Dornier Do.215 bombers, skimming the waves off Dover making for France. Attacked by Squadron Leader Malan, Pilot Officer Cobden and Pilot Officer Freebourne, together with Sergeant Hastings, they accounted for two of them. 54 Squadron, operating from Rochford, encountered some Bf.109's, and 'Jonnie' Allan and 'Al' Deere shared one of them. Pilot Officer Allan's Spitfire (R6812) was hit by enemy fire. He tried to reach Manston but crashed on the outskirts of Foreness and was killed.

As the attacks by the Luftwaffe increased, more squadrons were engaged in flying from the Forward Landing Grounds to concentrate up to twenty-eight squadrons in the south-east to meet the threat to ports such as Dover and Folkestone. Meanwhile, on the ground the airfields tried to carry on normal station routine:

"During the latter half of July and the beginning of August, the raids increased in intensity, and became more frequent — so much so that 'Yellow' and 'Red' alerts were of little significance and work continued as usual. Apart from the war in the air, the station had to be run the same as any small town or village. Food, Stores, Water, Gas, Electricity, Clothing, Pay, Defence Training and many other personnel services had to be organised by the Adjutant (Flight Lieutenant A. Smalley) and his staff." ('Bill' Grout)

On 27th July 604 Squadron was withdrawn to Middle Wallop in Hampshire and the following day Pilot Officer Lovell, of 41 Squadron, crash-landed his Spitfire (P9429) at Manston after combat with a Bf.109 over Dover. On 29th four more Spitfires of 41 Squadron crashed at Manston, the pilots being Flight Lieutenant Webster, Flying Officer Scott, Flying Officer MacKinnie and Pilot Officer Bennions — but all were uninjured.

On the last day of July, 74 Squadron was in action again over Dover, 'A' Flight orbiting at 20,000 ft. over Manston, before being joined by 'B' Flight and vectored to Dover. Upon arrival they found a combined force of Messerschmitt Me.110 fighter-bombers with a high level escort of Bf.109's. Two Spitfires were shot down near Folkestone, and that of Flight Lieutenant Kelly was damaged, but he managed to glide his aircraft (R6983) back to base. His adversary was also damaged, the pilot being wounded but made a crash-landing at Fecamp. Another Bf.109 was shot down making the tally for the action two Spitfires lost, two pilots killed and one Spitfire damaged for one Bf.109 down and one 'probable'.

Manston Operations board

65 Squadron arrived at 06.45 hrs at Manston and flew three sorties during the morning without making any interceptions; they carried out practice flying later in the day.

August started with routine patrols, but no excitement, apart from the crash on take-off of one of 41 Squadron's Spitfires on the 5th of the month. But three days later, 600 Squadron lost one of their Bristol Blenheims when two aircraft were carrying out practice with their radar over Ramsgate. One machine, flown by Flying Officer Boyde landed safely, but that of Flying Officer Grice was seen to drive out of cloud over the town, with its engines ablaze. The mid-day shoppers crowding the town saw the aircraft pull up as if to avoid crashing in the town centre, and the Blenheim dived into the sea outside the harbour killing Grice, Sergeant Kent and Aircraftman Warren. It was assumed that the Blenheim, whose outline could be mistaken for a Junkers Ju.88, could have been a victim of mistaken identity by a RAF fighter or a local 'ack-ack' battery. Comments were made that Pilot Officer Grice deserved an award for sacrificing himself and his crew to avoid crashing on Ramsgate, but none was given. Another of the squadron's aircraft was lost the following day when Flying Officer Bougtel suffered engine failure over Margate and baled out with his crewman, Sergeant Smith. 74 Squadron took part in an inconclusive battle over Margate when the town was attacked at about 14.00 hrs.

One witness to these events was eighteen-year-old Rosina Saxby, who was living with her family on the edge of Margate, overlooking the aerodrome. She

Parade at Manston during visit by General Smutts, South African Prime Minister — showing damage to hangars and buildings (Mr A.T. Gifford)

had started to keep a diary after seeing the troops being landed at Margate during the Dunkirk evacuation. Her entry for August 9th reads:

"Two sirens today, one in the afternoon, one in the evening. About 10.00 pm fourteen bombs were dropped on this town. Some fell on small houses, some in a church memorial garden, and were dug up on Saturday. Very heavy gunfire (from Manston) and we saw a plane come down, and the sheen lit up the sky; we thought it was a Jerry, but later learned to our great dismay that it was one of ours. The pilot was safe, he baled out. The German plane swooped down and we thought that the bombs were going to fall very near us, we heard them whistle when he released them. A few casualties were taken to hospital, and glass littered the streets from broken windows."

The two accidents involving 600 Squadron were not generally known on the station as security was very tight, Squadron Leader Grout makes this observation:

"Strangely enough we didn't hear about many of the incidents which took place at Manston, even though we were on the airfield. Unless you happened to be on guard duty or manning the defences, you didn't know half of what went on. There were always rumours, of course, but nothing definite was told us. I read about the Flying Officer Grice incident in the papers some time later."

The 11th August was another busy day for 74 Squadron, seeing them flying four sorties from dawn. The first of these was over Dover, where Pilot Officer Stevenson was shot down at 08.10 hrs, but landed by parachute in the sea and

94

attracted the attention of a MTB by firing his revolver. The next patrol, between 09.50 and 10.45 hrs, saw no engagements by the twelve aircraft patrolling in the Dover area. At 11.45 hrs eleven aircraft were dispatched to patrol over convoy 'Booty' passing Dover. They were being attacked by forty Me.110's, which formed a defensive circle when the Spitfires arrived. Pilot Officer Freebourne dived through the middle of the enemy circle, 'Sailor' Malan claimed two of them and 'Tubby' Mayne damaged two others. Because of trouble with the R/T, the remainder of the squadron did not hear the order to engage. Malan rejoined his colleagues to patrol over Dover, then attacked two more enemy aircraft, damaging one Bf.109 before being engaged himself by eight others. Ten more Bf.109's were sighted, and Malan went after them, but could not draw the attention of the other Spitfires to them, so he returned to Manston.

Just over an hour later 74 Squadron took off for their fourth patrol, this time with eight aircraft, to patrol Hawkinge. However, they were vectored to the north-east of Margate where they found ten Junkers Ju.87's with an escort of twenty Bf.109's.

The Messerschmitts dived for the cloud layer below to avoid combat and Malan, Freebourne, Stephen and Mungo-Park attacked. Freebourne downed one and Malan chased another to Cap Gris Nez before shooting it down into the sea. The results for the day were nine Bf.109's shot down and five Me.110's, for the loss of Pilot Officers Smith and Cobden.

The enemy turned his attention to coastal airfields on 12th August and Fighter Command was hard pressed to get into battle in time. The first heavy bombing attack on Manston came at 12.50 hrs when a mixed formation of Exp.Gp.210 Me.110's, escorted by Bf.109's attacked the airfield. Hurtling fast and low over the hangars from the direction of Ramsgate, they dropped some 150 high-explosive and incendiary bombs, pitting the airfield with craters, damaging two hangars and destroying the workshops formerly occupied by No. 3 School of Technical Training – all in the space of five minutes. So bad was the apparent effect, when viewed from the cockpits of the bombers, that the airfield was reported to be unserviceable, and was deleted from Luftwaffe maps. Foreign press reports, based on German sources, spoke of Manston being 'reduced to ashes'. In fact the airfield was only out of action for one day, although the runways had been pockmarked with over a hundred craters.

65 Squadron had arrived earlier in the morning and were still on the ground when the alarm was given, just as the bombs began to fall. The pilots were just preparing for take off, and a wild melée developed as the Spitfires raced across the airfield in an attempt to get airbourne. Flying Officer Wigg was sucked up by the blast of the bombs with his engine dead; Flight Lieutenant Jeffery Quill (later to become a test pilot for the makers of the Spitfire, Supermarine) managed to get off, with Pilot Officer 'Paddy' Finucane. The latter had just joined the squadron and had already been in action that morning, but climbed to 30,000 ft. after shaking off two persistent Bf.109's, and sighted twelve more. He dived and shot down the leading Bf.109 into the sea. Returning to Manston, Finucane

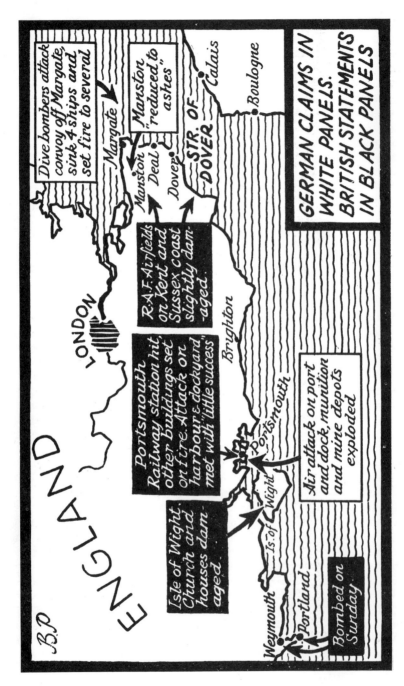

Press montage of German claims after raids on 12th August 1940 — Manston 'Reduced to Ashes' with British counter claim — both inaccurate! (Squadron Leader W.L. Grout)

'bagged' another Bf.109 over the airfield, and was well on his way to his eventual score of 32 enemy aircraft, and his promotion to Wing Commander.

54 Squadron had been on patrol nearby when the attack started, and 'Al' Deere had alerted Blue Section (Pilot Officer Colin Grey) which had tried to divert the bombers from their aiming point. They alone could not penetrate the fighter escort as the remainder of the squadron was en route to Dover to intercept another raid. Deere attacked a lone Bf.109 and chased it as far as Deal, before being ordered back to base. Although the Luftwaffe later announced that 65 Squadron had been destroyed, the Spitfires which did manage to take off joined 54 Squadron in attacking the Bf.109 escort, landing back at the airfield to dodge the bomb craters in the runway.

Miss Saxby's entry for the 12th August includes the following passage:

"One plane came over in the morning and made a ring (circled) over the different aerodromes, and later twenty to twenty-five German planes came over and bombed them. I watched them bomb Manston, and they seemed to swoop out of the sky, then dive down and as one came up, the next one dived down. They damaged the landing field and hangars at Manston, and on their flight out to sea bombed and machine gunned the men that had been working on the defence works in the fields (pillboxes)."

600 Squadron had been on patrol the night before and the pilots were dozing in the sunshine, their aircraft dispersed around the East Camp on the Ramsgate side of the airfield. These boys were members of the Royal Auxillary Air Force pre-war, and known as 'The Millionaires Mob' due to their penchant for fast cars and hand tailored uniforms. They were a mad lot, who were always up to some scheme or other, remembers 'Bill' Grout. "On one occasion they dismantled the C.O.'s Austin 7 and reassembled it in the Officers' Mess, and also ran curling championships in the mess, using chamber pots." However, they were soon in action with their 'home-made' defences consisting of stripped-down Browning machine guns mounted on poles, and shot down one of the Me.110's. Two of their Blenheim night-fighters were destroyed and one of their pilots, Flying Officer Duncan Smith, had a shock when he arrived back from leave in a Tiger Moth in the middle of the raid. Not having a radio on board, he had no warning of the goings on at Manston, but managed to land safely.

As though not satisfied with their mid-morning work, the Luftwaffe returned at 17.20 hrs. A formation of Dornier Do.17's dropped more bombs on the already shattered airfield when seventy of them flew in at 15,000 ft. Waiting for them were 56 Squadron who had been scrambled from Rochford to re-inforce the defences at Manston. They attacked the bombers after they had become separated from their escort of Bf.109's. Geoffrey Page engaged one of the fighters off Margate, but his Hurricane was shot down by a yellow-nosed Bf.109 and Page baled out to land in the sea some ten miles off the coast. Although there were two Air Sea Rescue launches based at Ramsgate, he was picked up by the Margate lifeboat 'J.B. Proudfoot', which had already rescued the crews of two trawlers.

Bristol Blenheim Mk.1.F's with Ventral Gun Packs, of 600 (City of London) Squadron. Royal Auxiliary Air Force, Manston 1940

These ships had been sunk when a convoy had been attacked off Margate at noon. This was the first concentrated attack on Manston, although the ground crews who serviced the fighters had suffered from the attentions of enemy fighters previously.

During the attack some 187 bombs had been dropped and for the majority of the personnel at the airfield the experience was something new and horrific. Stories of the effects on these men which have been given credance up until now, can be seen in a different light when the following account is considered. Squadron Leader Grout observes:

"It has been said in my presence on many occasions that morale at Manston in 1940 was very low, and that airmen cowered in dug-out shelters refusing to emerge for days. This is gross exaggeration and just is not true. The stories evolve around No. 12 Servicing Flight, the members of which did a magnificent job in servicing, re-arming and generally maintaining the many aircraft of the various squadrons during the summer of 1940. It consisted of highly trained Fitters, Riggers, Armourers, Drivers, etc. etc. all dedicated to their job of keeping the fighters in the air at all costs. During the height of the Battle, the ground staff suffered many casualties from enemy ground-straffing by Bf.109's and Me.110's, whilst our squadrons were being re-fuelled and re-armed. As a result, it is true that some of the Flight were reluctant to come out of shelter whilst this was going on. However our Squadron Commanders quickly devised a plan to keep one flight of fighters circling above, whilst the servicing was going on, then swopping places to re-fuel themselves."

Despite the constant alarms and excursions, the airmen still managed to find time to snatch some quick respite from the rigours of their life at Manston. L.A.C. Wallis recalls how he and his pals did this:

"Being in the Stores there was never a dull moment during the raids, under cover — then back to work. My closest pal was one Corporal Jack Finlay, the life and soul of the party. Whenever it was possible to have a break, we would wend our way, together with our civilian Stores Officer, to the 'Prospect Inn', on the Minster Road, for a quick one."

The 'Prospect Inn' was kept by a retired Army Officer and was the hostelry used by the airmen. The pilots and aircrew would repair to the 'Jolly Farmer', in Manston Village which was kept by a retired Warrant Officer at No. 3 School of Technical Training at Manston.

In spite of the surprise and the intensity of the bombing on August 12th, there was only one casualty, a civilian clerk, Mr Jackson, who was killed. He was the treasurer of the Isle of Thanet Branch of the Comrades of the RAF.

By dusk the clearing up was well under way, and the following morning saw fighters from No. 11 Group patrolling over the airfield to ward off more attacks. No. 1 Squadron was detached to three airfields in the south east, including Manston, for the next three days, and even the Blenheims of 600 Squadron were pressed into service to keep away the unwelcome attentions of the Luftwaffe. Between the 13th and 18th August, some thirty-four airfields and five Radar stations were attacked, and Hawkinge, Manston and several others were bombed on more than one occasion.

On 14th August a dozen Me.110's, escorted by sixteen Bf.109's evaded the defending fighters while they were engaged with a feint attack off Dover. Dive-bombing and machine gunning the remains of the buildings, the attackers destroyed four of the hangars in their attack at 13.00 hrs, but lost four of their number. One to a Bofors gun manned by the Army, another to the 'Heath Robinson' defences of 600 Squadron – a Hispano gun mounted on a tripod. One fighter, flown by Unterofficer Hans Steding, struck the ground with its wing and cartwheeled across the airfield. The hangar of 600 Squadron was burnt out, destroying four more of their aircraft, but the machine guns mounted on the crew-room roof accounted for another Me.110D. 74 Squadron was withdrawn from the airfield as things were getting extremely unpleasant, and the operations by fighters from the base was impracticable.

Corporal 'Charley' Green of the Hampshire Regiment based at Margate for coast defence was one of the Army personnel who helped defend Manston:

"We used to be posted up to Manston for anti-aircraft duties. I would take a section up to the aerodrome with a Bren gun, which was mounted on a tripod for use as an anti-aircraft gun. We were all round the edge of the airfield."

The next day the bomb-carrying Me.110's of Experimental Group 210 again visited Manston, when nine aircraft attacked at 12.10 hrs. However two of the enemy were destroyed – one by a Royal Artillery manned Bofors gun and another by 600 Squadron's ground mounted Hispano m/g. They were escorted by a dozen Bf.109's, which attacked the airfield with cannon and machine guns, destroying two Spitfires of 266 Squadron which had been evacuated from East-church. All the hard work of clearing up the airfield was undone and yet another hangar was partly wrecked in the East Camp, and sixteen personnel were killed or injured.

54 Squadron was in action again, after helping to defend Lympne from a dive-bombing attack, losing three aircraft and one pilot. 'Al' Deere was nearly

Station Admin Staff, Manston post September 1940 at 'Z' Point, Westgate. Flt Lt Willis (4th from left front row), Sgt Gifford (2nd from left), Cpl Shurland (1st from left)

(Mr A.T. Gifford)

shot down himself while chasing a Me.110 over the airfield when one of 600 Squadron's machine guns opened up at the enemy fighter just as Deere came in to land. Corporal Green remembers the incident thus:

> "One day when we were up there (at Manston) a Jerry came over very low, so low that we had difficulty getting the gun down to get him in the sights. The boys opened up, and instead of getting the Jerry, they hit the aircraft which was chasing him. The pilot landed safely as his aircraft was only damaged, but then he came over to the site, and he didn't half swear at them."

The 16th of August was another day of attacks on airfields, including Manston, where eight Bf.109's machine gunned the long suffering Blenheims of 600 Squadron, destroying one, and damaging two others, at 17.45 hrs. The night-fighter crews did some sterling work by helping re-fuel and re-arm the day fighters, after having been out on patrol themselves the previous night. Both 65 and 56 Squadrons were in action over the airfield earlier in the day, Pilot Officer Grahame being shot down in flames at 13.15 hrs over Manston, and Pilot Officer Pyman was posted as missing after combat in the same area.

There was a day's respite from attacks on the 17th, but it was common practice for night raiders to unload their remaining bombs on the airfield before chancing the Channel crossing. L.A.C. Len Wallis had his own way of dealing with these night raids, and it was to save his life:

"I think we spent many sleepless nights during this period, and either volunteered for extra duties, or stayed up as long as possible. I was in the NAAFI one night and had to stay in a shelter during the raid. When I returned to my room (Corporals were normally in charge of a barrack room, and had a little room at the end of the block) it was not there. A direct hit on the corner of the block had destroyed my room plus everything I had, except what I was wearing. I have often thought what a lucky lad I was going for a cup of tea to the NAAFI that night, I was normally a heavy sleeper. The next day I reported to the Clothing Store for a new outfit."

Early on the morning of 18th August, 54 Squadron was again moved forward to Manston. It was not a very welcome sight which greeted them this Sunday morning, only four buildings were tenable, water was cut off, and even water for shaving had to be obtained from the pre-war swimming pool behind the parade ground. 266 Squadron was there, without aircraft or equipment, and no means of replacing either. Only 600 Squadron continued to function, however the airfield could still be used for landings in an emergency and a Hurricane of 17 Squadron, flown by Sergeant Griffiths, made a forced landing there.

The airfield was attacked four times during the day by Me.110's, accompanied by Bf.109's, which straffed living quarters and the C.O.'s house (into which the administrative staff had been moved) with machine guns and cannon fire. Many casualties occurred, the worst attack being at 15.30 hrs when twelve Bf.109's rocketed over the base, straffing two Spitfires of 615 Squadron which were being serviced in the open. The ground crews were caught in the open without warning, one being killed and fifteen injured with broken limbs while re-fuelling and re-arming the Spitfires. Both aircraft were destroyed together with the Hurricane of 17 Squadron mentioned previously. However, 54 Squadron did manage to shoot down one Me.110 during the morning, when Oblt Wendien of 7(K)LG2 was killed after being attacked by five Spitfires at 3,000 ft. over the airfield.

Squadron Leader 'Bill' Grout recalls the trials and tribulations of the ground crews:

"The Germans also frequently straffed the ground crews whilst returning to the main camp for meals. An attempt to minimise this danger was made by 'staggering' the meal-times for the various flights and sections (10.30 hrs to 14.00 hrs). But the enemy had an uncanny knack of soon adapting their attacks to the new times."

The following is an extract from the Daily Routine Orders for RAF Manston quoting a signal received after the attacks of this particular day:

"850. ENEMY ATTACK – SUNDAY 18th AUGUST 1940
Group Commander wishes all ranks RAF, Army and WAAF to be congratulated on their good discipline and calm behaviour under heavy fire when enemy attacked your aerodrome on Sunday August 18th. Also to commend

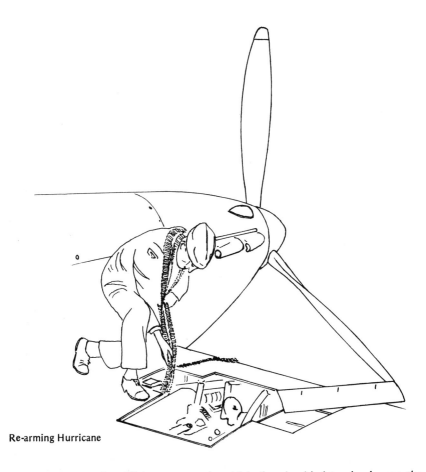

Re-arming Hurricane

all ranks on the efficient manner in which they buckled to clearing up the damage caused by the enemy. Your organisation and good discipline undoubtedly contributed to the relatively small number of casualties as a result of heavy attacks under which ground personnel displayed the fine offensive spirit that our fighter pilots have been demonstrating in air combat. (11 Group H.Q. signal A/117 dated 22/8/40)

signed A. J. Smalley
Flight Lieutenant (Adjutant)
RAF Station, Manston."

'Bill' Grout has retained his copy of this signal to this day.

Air Vice Marshal Park decided, despite the constant attacks on the Forward Landing Grounds, to keep his fighters from No. 11 Group operational from Manston and Hawkinge, so that attacks by the Luftwaffe could be broken up before penetrating too far inland. During the following days a spell of bad weather prevented the enemy from assembling any large raids, and they had to be content with high-altitude sweeps and a few sharp fighter-bomber attacks against Manston, and some scattered bombing raids.

Just after 14.00 hrs on 20th August that airfield was again straffed, but caused very little damage and no casualties, apart from one Blenheim of 600 Squadron which was hit by cannon shells. Two days later there was another raid by fighters, but with no great effect, apart from precipitating the withdrawal of 600 Squadron to Hornchurch which was mooted after this latest attack.

L.A.C. Len Wallis had a narrow squeak during one mid-morning attack by Bf.109's:

"Apart from the night raids, most of the day raids came at lunch-time. I was in the main dining room on one such raid. Everyone dashed out to the underground shelters. One entrance was opposite the dining room door with the main camp road between. Arriving at the shelter I discovered that, in the panic to get out, I had forgotten my knife, fork and spoon in the dining room. Amid protests from my mates I left the shelter, crossed the road and retrieved my cutlery. I was on my way back and halfway across the road when bullets began to fly from three German aircraft which started to straff just as I got to the road. In spite of this I crawled to the entrance of the shelter, but was unaware of the risk I had taken. After the raid was over I learned that one airman and a civilian had been killed.

"It was on the same day that we had to fill in bomb craters on the airfield, and I could well imagine what it must have been like at the front in the First World War."

'Bill' Grout also has a story to tell concerning the filling in of craters:

"There was a detachment of Royal Engineers detailed to assist in filling in the craters in the runways, but everybody turned out to help. The only instance I can recall regarding any airmen remaining in the shelters built in the chalk cliffs for several days, was when a party of recruits were sent down from Blackpool Recruits Centre to help with the repair to the damage to the grass airfield. As they were proceeding from the railway station to Manston, a raid started. They were all young inexperienced recruits, and apparently were directed to the old railway tunnel built in the Ramsgate Cliffs. (From the old Harbour Station to Dumpton.) They were given food and drink by the local residents until such time as they were collected by the RAF (service Police) and returned to Blackpool. I understand that, as a result of this episode, two senior NCO's who were originally in charge of the party, were court-martialled (for abandoning their charges and hopping back on the train, having heard of the reputation of Manston as a 'hot-spot').

Before the evacuation of 600 Squadron could be put into effect, Manston was to undergo its worst baptism of fire. This was 24th August and it was effectively to end operations there until the following year.

40mm Bofors anti-aircraft gun

Saturday 24th August opened with 264 Squadron being ordered forward from their base in Yorkshire to Hornchurch in Essex at 0.500 hrs to help defend Manston from early morning raids. An almost continuous stream of bombers and fighters were plotted assembling over Calais to join together in three close formations. The first raid developed at 08.00 hrs and the Defiant two-seater, turret fighters took off to intercept some Bf.109's. During the action Flight Lieutenant Campbell Calquoun mistakenly joined two enemy fighters thinking them to be his formation. For his trouble he was attacked and the enemy ignited the Very cartridges in the fuselage of his aircraft and he landed with them exploding like a mobile firework display.

The remainder of the squadron was ordered to land back at Hornchurch, but hardly had they time to get out of their aircraft when they were instructed to return to Manston. During the mid-morning two separate bomber wings, escorted by Bf.109's, missed their main target at Manston and dropped their bombs near Canterbury. A few minutes later a Heinkel wing headed towards Dover, with strong fighter escort. 54 Squadron was one of the units of Spitfires and Hurricanes which failed to reach the bombers, but shot down two Bf.109's, damaging another for the loss of Pilot Officer Campbell. The bombers turned their attentions to Ramsgate, dropping some sixty bombs on the airport and a further 150 on the town itself.

When the Defiants arrived back from Hornchurch, nine aircraft landed while one section led by Flight Lieutenant Barham circled above to keep an eye out for sneak attacks. Seven of the Defiants had been re-fuelled and re-armed by 12.50 hrs and were about to take off when twenty Junkers Ju.88's, escorted by a swarm of Bf.109's swept in from the sea. As the bombs were falling on the airfield, the Defiants desperately struggled to get into the air, but in the whirling mass of fighters and bombers above the runway, three of their number were shot down. But the Junkers spent too long over the aerodrome and on their withdrawal across the Channel the Defiants pounced on them. Flight Lieutenant Barham, with his gunner, Baker, shot down one Ju.88 of Stab II/KG76, south of the airfield, killing Major Morick and his crew. Another was downed by Garrin and Ash, while a third was rammed by Whitely and Turner five minutes later. Squadron Leader Hunter, C.O. of 264 Squadron, and gunner Pilot Officer King shot down another, but while chasing another bomber towards France, were themselves shot down south east of the airfield in Defiant N4535, and both killed. Defiant L6966, flown by Pilot Officer Jones and crewed by Pilot Officer Postery were shot down east of Manston at 13.20 hrs, followed by Flying Officer Shaw and Sergeant Berry five minutes later.

As the bombers swept over the airfield, the ground defences came into operation. At the dispersal area of 600 Squadron every kind of weapon was used. A Vickers machine gun on a pole, rifles, Very pistols were fired at the raiders and even clods of earth and lumps of chalk were hurled by those without any other means of retaliating. In all, five of the Ju.88's were shot down and two Bf.109's, but the price had been high as extensive damage had been done to the airfield. The remaining hangars had been demolished, aircraft at dispersal and the armoury were all left blazing, and the airfield covered with craters and unexploded bombs. Manston was completely isolated although telephone and teleprinter lines remained intact, but few buildings were habitable. The crew operations room of 600 Squadron had been hit, and its circuits severed and the base was a shambles.

'Bill' Grout was trying to catch up on some much-needed sleep when the attack took place, and one of the first bombs to fall struck Bungalow B.4 where he was in bed:

"I was extremely lucky, inasmuch as the blast blew the heavy door of my room across the bed, and I was buried underneath the debris. I eventually managed to dig myself out, and assisted by the casualties from Bungalow C.5 (opposite) then proceeded to the main guard-room where my fellow Sergeant, Bob Sherwood, was Guard Commander. I must have looked a rare old 'sight' as one of the soldiers on guard duty threatened to shoot me! He was calmed down however, and I was talking to a couple of Margate policemen in the roadway alongside the billets, when three Bf.109's screamed down out of the sun with guns blazing. I dived headlong into a space between two walls forming the entrance to one of the bungalows, and was quickly followed by the two policemen, who practically squashed me alive.

"I later discovered that all my belongings were scattered around the area, including the squadron cricket team's equipment, pads, stumps etc. which had ended up in a nearby tree."

The Margate Fire Brigade was soon on the scene, as the station fire fighters could not cope with the many fires raging all over the airfield. Under the direction of Chief Officer Albert Twyman, civilian and RAF personnel fought to control the conflagration and evacuate weapons and stores from the damaged buildings. At the same time, civilians from Ramsgate also moved in to help 'evacuate' tools from the workshops, formerly housing No. 3 School of Technical Training.

During the afternoon, while squadrons were re-fuelling on the ground, a big raid was plotted by the ever-watching radar stations over Le Havre. The attack came just before tea-time on Manston, Hornchurch and North Weald. Living quarters were badly damaged and all telephone and teleprinter circuits had been severed between Manston and Group and Sector Control after the previous raid. The GPO maintenance inspector was informed and he brought two fitters to commence the task of getting the essential connections re-established. Despite the continuous explosion of delayed action bombs, these three men worked alongside a large un-exploded bomb at the bottom of a large crater. They managed to reconnect the essential lines within two hours, and to complete all the circuits by the following day — there being some 248 separate connections to be made. The firemen also worked continuously to extinguish the fires in the hangars and stores for the next two days. Fireman Fred Watson manned a pump at the only underground tank available, alongside which was an unexploded bomb. This later detonated leaving a large crater, but for his heroism, Fireman Watson was awarded the George Medal, also awarded to Chief Officer Twyman for his work at Manston. The M.T. section had also been hit. 'Bill' Grout remembers:

"Anybody who could drive was ordered to take a vehicle and 'get the hell out of it' to save them being set alight.

"I can also recall meeting the Station Chaplain, Squadron Leader (The Rev.) King, and accompanying him to the main shelter beneath the old Parade Square. This was full of airmen, not assigned to any specific duties, and the Padre spoke to them all with a cheery word. They were quite cheerful and morale was high — singing, arguing, playing cards etc.

"The NAAFI Manageress came running to us to say that she could not find any of her girls in the building. We found them safe and well in the Beer Cellar. They were quickly taken away from the camp by transport, as many unexploded bombs lay around the NAAFI building."

Rosina Saxby's diary entry for 24th August reveals that it was not only Manston which suffered from the attentions of the Luftwaffe:

"A day of continuous air raids. All day onslaught by bombers escorted by fighters. Manston and other aerodromes in E. Kent were attacked in the morning. Ramsgate was bombed and the gasworks and other buildings hit. Dover was also hit, but little damage done. Considerable damage was done at

Manston to the buildings. Ramsgate suffered heavily as a large number of high explosives and incendiary bombs were dropped. We had five sirens in all down here."

Her entry for Monday 26th gives a more detailed picture:

"My friend who was at Ramsgate said that Saturday was terrible; there are hardly any houses there that haven't been damaged in one way or another. She also said that it seemed that all their houses were on fire. Soldiers and ARP men were machine gunned as they went to help with the rescue work."

It would not have been surprising if the citizens of Ramsgate had blamed their misfortune on the proximity of Manston aerodrome, but a note from 'Bill' Grout gives his impressions.

"I never at any time heard any adverse comments regarding the proximity of Manston Airfield and the consequent danger to the town. In off duty moments, many of the hostelries proved a pleasant divergence from duty, and all were made very welcome. The townsfolk were keen to show their appreciation of all RAF personnel . . . Ramsgate was bombed (and shelled) many times — on 24th August, it was calculated that 500 bombs were dropped on the town destroying over 1,000 homes.

"It must be remembered of course, that all non-essential people and children were evacuated early in 1940, and those that remained; i.e. Policemen, Firemen, Waterboard, Coastguard, Publicans etc, were all regarded as part of 'the team'."

After the situation at Manston had been reported to Fighter Command, it was decided to evacuate the airfield except for emergency landings. It is said that when Churchill was told about this he said: "Such a disgrace must never occur again". 600 Squadron, or the remains thereof, were posted to Hornchurch, together with the remnants of 264 Squadron, and 12 Servicing Flight had to camp out in the woods near the aerodrome until they were disbanded and posted to various destinations in the U.K. 'Bill' Grout was also evacuated:

"Later that evening, I moved my staff, records, etc. by lorry under cover of darkness, down to an empty house in Westgate. I was given charge of a Standard van, and the following day (Sunday) I was able to obtain ample rations from the Army Catering Depot at Dreamland, Margate. I also returned to Manston to find it practically derelict and evacuated — some of the squadron personnel were camping out in the woods at Quex Park. Whilst on the camp one or two delayed action bombs exploded in the former Technical Training School workshops.

"On 2nd September, the Headquarters Staff moved into Streete Court Infants School, Westgate, including the new C.O. Squadron Leader Manton. I slept on a landing floor, and others made do in various ways. The facilities, provided for very small children, were a trifle inadequate (low level toilets and basins meant shaving whilst on ones knees, and hot water had to be

Heinkel He.59B air sea rescue seaplane on Walmer Beach, after being forced down near Goodwin Sands on 9th July 1940 by Spitfires of 54 Squadron from Manston. Painted white overall, with red crosses and tail stripe. Code letters D-ASUO.   (Norman Cavell)

Station HQ and Technical Training School, RAF Manston, c.1929. No. 9 Squadron Virginias in the south west corner.   (RAF Museum)

'humped' upstairs in kettles and buckets). But there were several pubs in the area which helped. The Officer's Mess was established in a large house on the opposite side of the road. Streete Court was officially known as 'Z' Point.''

The long suffering defenders of Manston managed to find an excuse for the many attacks on the aerodrome, even if it was only a rumour. Corporal Green remembers:

"There was some talk about one of the officers at Manston being a Fifth Columnist, but whether there was any truth in that I don't know. But we did hear talk about it when we were up there. The story was that this officer used to flash torches. When the aerodrome was bombed badly it was supposed to have been this officer who signalled to the Germans."

'Bill' Grout also remembers similar rumours, but about the proprietor of the Accacia Cafe alongside the Margate Road, frequented by the airmen. He also remembers that the true reason, according to rumours circulating at the time, for the communications being cut after the morning raid on 24th August, was that it was the work of a fifth columnist. These rumours are hardly surprising when a couple of real spies had been arrested on the aerodrome just before the war.

During the main attack on 24th August, Sergeant Ronnie Hanbury, of 610 Squadron at Biggin Hill, a veteran of Dunkirk operations, attacked an enemy bomber off Ramsgate from 12,000 ft. to sea level, also shooting down a Bf.109. He was later awarded the DFM for shooting down five aircraft in one day. 510 Squadron also claimed a Bf.109 during the raids on Manston, but despite the devastation at the airfield only seven persons were killed during the attacks.

On 26th August, while the base was packing up to move, Spitfires of 54 Squadron, led into combat by Flight Lieutenant Saunders, intercepted a group of thirty Dorniers over Manston at 18,000 ft, escorted by three times as many Bf.109's. The RAF fighters attacked and shot down a Bf.109E-1 of 1/JG52 near Ramsgate, and were then joined by 610 Squadron which got another Messerschmitt. 264 Squadron was also operating in the area, orbiting between Deal and Herne Bay, where they were attacked by fifty Bf.109's after engaging twelve Dorniers. Flight Lieutenant Barham, acting as C.O. in place of Squadron Leader Hunter, was shot down and baled out off Margate. His gunner was posted as missing, together with another gunner, and two more of the squadron's aircraft were lost. However one Dornier of 7/KG.3 was damaged in combat over the North Foreland, Lt. Eggemann being killed together with two of his crew.

Two days later, Manston still had a spark of life, 54 Squadron flying in from Hornchurch each morning to land trying to avoid the areas marked with little yellow flags indicating unsafe ground. Large formations of enemy fighters carried out sweeps over Kent during the day, and while attacking a Bf.109 over Herne Bay, 'Al' Deere was shot down, baled out and landed in a plum tree alongside the Canterbury—Gillingham road. During the afternoon the Prime Minister visited

Manston Airfield 1980. The only operational station in Kent. Manston is the home of Air Sea Rescue Helicopters, the RAF Fire Fighting School, and is a staging post for longer flights.
(Len Pilkington)

south east Kent, calling in at Manston en route to see the bomb damage at Ramsgate. He found the base barely serviceable, craters everywhere and unexploded bombs marked with red flags all over the aerodrome. No attempt had been made to carry out any work on filling the craters on the runways, and as he walked silently among the piles of rubble he was deep in thought. Was it worth keeping Manston open, how to get it operational again, he couldn't be seen to be giving way to the Luftwaffe. After his visit the first organised Airfield Servicing Parties were sent to aerodromes to keep runways clear and craters filled, and 54 Squadron continued to fly forward each morning to the airfield, still covered with a thin layer of chalk dust.

Len Wallis recalls the Prime Minister's visit, and the evacuation of the airfield:

"The day after we had suffered the continuous raids, the radio news reported that Lord Haw Haw had said that Manston had been razed to the ground. It was pretty bad, so bad that that afternoon we made preparations for the evacuation of the airfield. Most of us were moved to Quex Park, near Birchington, where we slept under the trees for a couple of nights. But Mr Churchill made a visit to Manston and the following day we were back in camp getting things organised again."

On 2nd September the main camp had been evacuated, 266 Squadron having gone two days previously, and 264 Squadron had been withdrawn from operations in the south east after losing two more of their Defiants. They were to return later in the year to Gravesend as a night-fighter unit. The Luftwaffe still made occasional raids on Manston during the remainder of the Battle of Britain, but the aircraft parked alongside the runways were only cleverly constructed timber and canvas dummies. Squadron Leader Manton set about the task of restoring the facilities at the base in preparation for the planned operations to carry the fight to the enemy after the Battle of Britain had been won, and the danger of invasion past.

Manston now became an emergency landing ground for bombers; Leading Aircraftman Len Wallis was involved in this period of the Station's history:

"I was in charge of the fire crew on the RAF Fire Tender. We were based at the Air Traffic Control, and received our orders from the Air Traffic Controller. We had to deal with all sorts of aircraft which had been forced to land through lack of fuel, or were shot up and crippled by enemy fire. I remember quite clearly being told to stand by for a bomber which had been hit by enemy fire, with casualties. When she came in and made a crash-landing, fuel was pouring from the tanks, but luckily the aircraft did not catch fire; one crew member was taken off in the ambulance, but how badly injured I do not know.

"It always amazed me that so much safety routine that pilots went through under normal conditions were ignored. I have seen Manston aerodrome littered with crippled planes, and aircraft landing and taking off all over the place, plus refuellings going on as well. No wonder we won the Battle of Britain."

Thus closes the story of the part which RAF Manston played in the Battle of Britain, an important part for the pilots who operated from there; landed to re-fuel and re-arm; or found the airfield a haven when damaged or wounded out over the waters of the English Channel. Despite the difficulty of operating an aerodrome so close to the bases of the Luftwaffe fighters and bombers, for which Manston suffered almost continuous attack during August 1940, the decision to keep the airfield operational as long as possible must have been justified. Not for Manston the glory of Biggin Hill, still remembered as the 'Battle of Britain' airfield, but the work of the pilots, ground crews, defenders and administrative staff and civilians at Manston was just as important as at any other airfield, and many of them made the ultimate sacrifice.

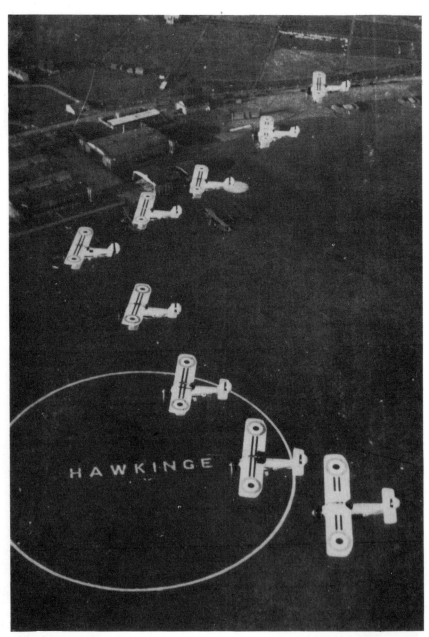

Sinskin 111a's 25 (F) Squadron flying over Hawkinge aerodrome in 1929. The identification circle can still be seen today from the air.

Chapter Six

RAF HAWKINGE

By Roy S. Humphreys

Under a lifeless grey sky in December 1961, Royal Air Force Hawkinge overlooking the town of Folkestone finally closed down, and with its closure went fifty-four years of aviation history. The pomp and ceremony to mark such a sad occasion, the guard of honour — RAF Bands — hauling down the Ensign for the last time — the speeches, pursued its inevitable course and, with the last bugle note fading into the distance the station ceased to exist.

Since that December day the old aerodrome has deteriorated into a state of decay. Buildings, once proud and immaculate have become dilapidated while more than half of the grass airfield, surrounded by broken fences and a cracked perimeter track, have returned to farmland where cattle graze and wheat crops flourish.

It began its existence before the 1914-18 war, when a Dutch pioneer aviator rented a small field just West of the village where he built an experimental flying machine. Dubbed the 'Mayfly', and built of welded tube, mutton cloth and miles of stranded wire, the machine never actually got off the ground. However, had it not been for the Dutchman's meagre efforts, that particular field might never have been selected by the Royal Flying Corps for a landing ground, in 1915.

Such modest beginnings were typical of most early aerodromes and the Barnhouse Flying field, as it was called then, with three Bessoneau hangars 'in situ', provided maintenance and refueling facilities for aircraft en route to France. By 1917, more permanently constructed buildings were being erected and the whole project became known as the 'Aeroplane Despatch Section Hawkinge', where the pungent aroma of castor oil, the sound of whirring propellors and spluttering engines brought a new fascination to the village. Those early sounds and signs of military aviation were to last for over four decades, during which not only did aircraft design and military air power alter considerably, but also, through strategic locality, the aerodrome became a vital link in our defence system.

In the post-war resettlement period the Royal Air Force front-line strength of over 3,000 aircraft had, by the dawn of a new decade, withered to just a few squadrons, although defence of the Realm was still important. For one thing we had clashed with the French over the Ruhr. Nevertheless, in recognition of this obvious danger, and in addition to our overseas commitments, a Home Defence Air Force was mustered which brought to Hawkinge No. 25 Squadron. Commanded by Sqdn. Ldr. Sir Norman Leslie, it reassembled its equipment from storage and their Sopwith Snipe fighters were soon flying around the Folkestone area.

By 1927, the squadron had returned to Hawkinge from San Stefano, Turkey, where they had been involved with the Chanak crises. During their absence two

The Hawker Fury 1's of 'C' Flight 25 (F) Squadron ('Flight')

Pilot Officer Pat Burke 25 (F) Squadron, on Watch Office duty at RAF Hawkinge 1937
(Burke)

114

other fighter squadrons had reformed at the aerodrome, but had since left. It was this period in RAF history which became the most colourful with squadron aircraft being daubed with unit insignias. Unortunately the Hawkinge-based squadron was given two black lines in parallel, 'Bars in Sinister' the adjutant had called them.

In subsequent years the squadron changed their aircraft as new designs were introduced. After the Snipe came the Gloster Grebe of the mid-twenties, then came the ponderous Armstrong Whitworth Siskin, an all-weather machine with a new fangled heated cockpit. The Siskin was replaced in the early 'thirties by the Sidney Camm designed Hawker Fury Interceptor, later up-dated as the Super Fury. It is the era of the Fury fighters that is specially remembered for their magnificent synchronised formation flying techniques. Individual flying expertise was proudly symbolic of peace-time RAF training. But there were occasions, of course, when rule-book flying was abandoned by the aerobatically minded pilot. On those occasions local farmers became targets for low-level light-hearted flying abuse. The tranquility of meadow and country lane was often shattered by snarling, high-powered aero engines. Nevertheless, the Officers Mess ante-room displayed a variety of silver cups and trophies as squadron professionalism increased.

The incomparable Fury gave way to the Hawker Demon, two-seated fighter, then came the Gloster Gladiator and finally the Bristol Blenheim medium bomber. It was the Blenheim which caused the squadron's move from Hawkinge, for they were quite unsuited to operate on grass. They left behind them No. 2 Army Co-operation squadron who had shared aerodrome facilities since 1934. Initially they used the Hawker Audax two-seater aircraft which they later changed for Hawker Hectors which, in turn, were replaced by the Westland Lysander.

Inevitably, peace-time flying became just a memory when Great Britain declared war on Germany in September 1939. Gone were the silver bi-planes of yesteryear. It had been an adventure for the young men, seeking excitement in an elite force. But one could not help wondering if they had absorbed the hours of instruction, for they were soon to have their confidence tested.

Aerodrome defence suddenly became all important. Army officers of various rank arrived to advise on matters concerning machine-gun sites, trenches, dug-outs, A.A. guns, and where sandbags should be placed to deflect blast. Last, but by no means least, thousands of gallons of camouflage paint transformed the aerodrome.

From out of snow-leaden skies came the first eight-gun fighters ever to use the aerodrome. They were the Hurricanes of No. 3 Squadron which, in the first snows of winter, began operating the daily Channel patrols. It seemed that the aerodrome was now ready for Hitler's war — a war which was drawing ever closer to England. But someone, somewhere, thought differently. The Hurricanes left, and in their place came hundreds of airmen to join a newly formed Recruiting Pool.

Probably even more bizarre was the sudden arrival of Queen Mary trailers

Hawker Audax K.3718 of No. 2 Army Co-operation Squadron seen at RAF Hawkinge 1935
(Stansfeld)

This shot of Westland Lysander L.4687, piloted by Flight Lieutenant Stansfeld, was taken at RAF Hawkinge on the arrival of the aircraft from Westlands. It was the first Lysander to operate with 2 (AC) Squadron. (Stansfeld)

loaded with dismantled aircraft and equipment belonging to No. 1 Pilotless Aircraft Unit. No one could understand the reasoning behind the move. Someone said it was a new secret weapon. However, improved weather conditions in February, allowed a couple of boffins from the RAE Farnborough, to erect aerial pylons, electrical apparatus and all sorts of wireless devices. Eventually, a Queen Wasp pilotless aircraft was flying around Folkestone at varying heights and speeds.

Pat Osborne, one of the technical wizards involved, recalls his stint at Hawkinge. "I remember," he said, "it was the time when unarmed Tiger Moths were flying up and down the Channel coastline in a strategical bid to bluff Goering about our air strength."

"An Army Co-operating squadron had recently moved in to Hawkinge from nearby Lympne, and they were operating Lysanders every day. So I gathered A.A. gunners had plenty of targets to aim at, although fortunately, they had not yet become 'trigger-happy'. I often wondered afterwards if we, in any way, contributed to Goering's confusion!"

At the time of the Dunkirk evacuation a special briefing room was established at the aerodrome in a building called the Haskard Target, where No. 22 Army Co-operation Group ultimately became responsible for supplying our beleaguered troops at Calais. It was here also that Air Vice Marshal Blount commanded the HQ called 'Back Component', which dealt with the many complexities of the evacuation. As a back-up operation when German military positions constantly changed by the hour, our medium bombers operated out of Hawkinge with fighter escort to attack the enemy positions. At the height of the evacuation period Hawkinge became host to hundreds of fighters — the Hurricanes and Spitfires, the Lysanders of the Army Co-op units, the medium bombers such as Blenheims and Battles, and even the Hawker Hectors used as a last resort in dropping supplies over France.

The Battle of Britain was about to begin. It was now that Hawkinge was to become famous along with other Kent fighter airfields. Once again under the control of Fighter Command, the coastal aerodrome, a satellite of the Biggin Hill sector station, was to prove invaluable to our defence system. Luftwaffe activity gradually increased over Southern England from June onwards. Our defending fighter squadrons increased their daily sorties and Hawkinge received the Hurricanes and Spitfires from dawn till dusk. Aerial battles, at anything from 2,000 to 20,000 feet, were commonplace in that summer of 1940, and many exploits of individual combat are now legends in the annals of historical documents. It was, I am sure, the last period of close aerial combat one was ever likely to witness.

The fighter pilots taking part in that epic battle, and only one third of the 3,000 participants actually bore the brunt of the fighting, were reckoned to be men of superior qualities backed by excellent training, equipment and leadership. Such a combination laced with courage and aggression surely gave them a buoyant invincibility.

Main Entrance and Guard Room RAF Station Hawkinge

RAF Parade Ground, Hawkinge

118

Quite apart from Log-Book entries, recorded statistics have proved without doubt our fighters were often outnumbered and stretched to the limit of their endurance. They were hard pressed to ward off the preliminary convoy attacks in the Channel long before Goering unleashed his aerial armada upon the mainland.

At Hawkinge the day's events usually began at 5.0 am, when the first detached squadron of aircraft were preparing to land. Those squadrons taking part in 'scrambles' from the aerodrome included Nos. 501, 32, 610, 72, 64, 79, 615 and 245, usually orientated to maintain standing patrols and anti-aircraft affiliation duties as well as the ever-increasing scrambles. It was an every day occurrence now to see fighters crashing on the airfield. The pilots were wrestling with damaged machines, blasted by cannon and machine-gun fire. Wings and ailerons, fuselage and rudders were torn to shreds. Overheating engines belched black smoke and undercarriages failed to lock in the 'down' position. The resulting crashes were catastrophic. Fire Tender and Ambulance crews had never experienced such confusion, not even in training.

The station electrician remembered one crashing Spitfire which hovered over the airfield like a Sparrow Hawk, before coming to grief at the very edge of the field.

". . . he flew right through the fence . . . and the wire wound round his propeller like cotton on a bobbin . . . the Spitfire tipped up on its nose and the wheels collapsed. The pilot was wearing a dark blue uniform of the Fleet Air Arm."

That was almost certainly Sub. Lt. D. Paul, of No. 64 squadron.

Another eye witness recalls seeing the demise of No. 79 Squadron's C.O., Sqdn. Ldr. Joslin, who with the rest of his unit had scrambled from Hawkinge.

". . . I was walking in a field about a mile from Elms Vale, Dover, when I saw a squadron of Hurricanes climbing into the sky . . . it was obvious they had just taken off from Hawkinge. But someway behind the remainder was one solitary Hurricane trying to catch up . . . but he never did. The next thing I remember is the sound of machine-guns . . . and the Hurricane I had been watching just blew up. There was a big flash . . . then I saw just little bits falling out of the sky. Nothing else. The other Hurricanes had not noticed because they kept on climbing.

The 'Gerry' . . . one of their Messerschmitts, banked round over Church Hougham and flew out to sea . . . I could see him quite clearly then . . . but never noticed him before he started to open fire on the Hurricane!"

That same squadron lost two more pilots the following day when Plt. Off. Wood crashed into the English Channel in flames, and Flg. Off. Mitchell died in his burning Hurricane near Dover.

With so much activity going on the anti-aircraft gun crews had become 'trigger-happy'. That particular term had been explained to me some years later by one of them, who wrote,

German reconnaissance photograph of RAF Hawkinge, taken in July 1941, showing the bomb damage of the 1940 air raids (Brenzett Museum)

". . . sometimes it was utterly confusing to keep up with unidentifiable, twisting blurred shapes at varying heights and angles of incidence . . . there were . . . I must admit, times when we fired at everything and anything which came within our range. We often put up a formidable barrage of shells . . . enough to deter the most courageous of men!"

That statement will bear out the many laconic Log-Book entries, 'Hit by our own guns'. There was one pilot who had managed to get back to Hawkinge, after being hit by our own A.A. guns over Dover, who stood swearing at his wrecked Spitfire before it blew up!

Tragedies associated with operational airfields are many and that which befell No. 141 Squadron at Hawkinge, in July 1940, will probably never be forgotten. Surviving pilots, whether of the Battle of Britain period, or at any other time, will have mixed feelings, some affectionate, others horrific, due to the traumas of their own particular conflict, personally experienced when operating from the aerodrome.

No. 141 Squadron, flying the Defiant fighter, had never been in action before that day in question — the 19th. Their initiation began just after noon when they scrambled to a point in mid-Channel. Here, as history records, they were bounced from out of the sun by the famous Richthofen Gerschwader, one of the crack German fighter units of that time. All the Defiants were hit in the first assault and, of the nine machines scrambled, only four got back to Hawkinge. The squadron's first action of the war ended in complete disaster with four pilots, six gunners and seven aircraft lost.

It was on August 12th, when Fighter Command was to experience its most intense day since the air war began, and when RAF Hawkinge was attacked for the first time. This was the start of Reichmarshal Goering's fierce airfield attacks, the softening up process in preparation of Hitler's Adler Tag (Eagle Day) offensive. The first air assault began early with Dover being bombed at 7.30 a.m., then five radar stations in Kent and Sussex were hit around 9.0 a.m. At mid-day, RAF Manston, the forward aerodrome near Ramsgate, received its first of many raids that later proved so devastating.

When Dover was being hit the Hawkinge personnel had been up and about for two hours, preparing to receive the first squadron of fighters on detachment. Although the plotting tables at Bently Priory, the heart of Fighter Command, were covered with coloured discs and markers, indicating the state of the fighting, no fighter squadron appeared at the aerodrome.

Soldiers of the 6th Buff's Regiment manning the machine-gun nests around the airfield perimeter, became fidgety. Everyone else seemed to be in action except them. A telephone rang somewhere, and a Very-Light flare shot up into the air above the Watch Office. At last No. 32 Squadron had been ordered down to Hawkinge and they were over the aerdrome like a cloud of locusts. The gunners heaved a sigh of relief as they watched the Hurricanes land and taxi to dispersals.

The fire truck and pump of the Auxiliary Fire Service in the village of Hawkinge 1940

Squadron Leader Michael Crossley, DFC., who was C.O. of No. 32 Squadron in those days, wrote ". . . we often found ourselves at Hawkinge from time to time for a short spell until relieved by another squadron from some other station such as Hornchurch — North Weald — Kenley or Biggin Hill. For us the greatest thing was not to be on dawn shift for after filling up with tea and a wad we often fell asleep again in the 'readiness' marquee. Sometimes our relieving squadron never arrived. It was then I used to ring up 'Ops' and ask diffidently if there was anything 'on-the-board' . . . if the answer was negative then I wanted to know where our relieving squadron had got to!"

On August 12th they were not relieved and the pilots sat around in groups watching the vapour trails strung out across the blue sky like shredded cotton wool. By 2.30 p.m., they were racing for their Hurricanes, heaving their parachutes on and climbing into their cockpits.

Mike Crossley remembered an incident which was not untypical of those hasty scrambles at Hawkinge. He wrote,

"When there was a reasonable early warning, pride precluded us from taking off in any other way but in tight formation. But there was the occasion when a sergeant pilot got so excited, rushing to catch up, that as he turned his aircraft into position for take off, he inadvertently knocked-off the gun safety catch, caught his glove in it, and loosed off a three-second broadside which smashed a row of windows in a hangar!"

122

But to get back to the 12th, it was close on 5.0 p.m. when No. 32 Squadron was scrambled for the second time. Also at that precise time fifteen JU88 bombers of II/KG76 were, at no more than 5,000 feet, making for Dungeness point where they split into two separate groups, one group heading inland while the other altered course towards Folkestone.

When the German raiders began their shallow dive on the aerodrome, Alan Harvey, a signalman of 2nd London Infantry Brigade, was sitting in a trench fiddling with a wireless receiver and trying to raise Brigade HQ. His earphones muffled the sound of hostile aero-engines. The first he knew of the attack was when huge clods of earth straddled his trench.

High explosive bombs and incendiaries were scattered across the airfield. The station workshop went up with a terrific bang, as did the equipment store, for both had received direct hits. Another building seemed to erupt from inside. Ammunition began to explode sending white-hot bullets in all directions. The ground shook under the detonations. Brick walls collapsed and telegraph poles and trees were uprooted.

Arthur Hall, a civilian employee, recalls:

"Everyone dived for cover — under hedges and vehicles, into dugouts and trenches. I was quite near a slit trench up by the Gibraltar Lane and, with about a dozen airmen, ran towards it. I got there first and dived headlong into it . . . everyone else fell on top of me . . . I couldn't move a muscle — I was pinned to the floor. I remember thinking . . . this is it . . . I shall be buried alive!"

Another witness to the first raid was Marion McNeill, a WAAF wireless operator attached to the then, top secret 'Y' Service Unit. She wrote,

". . . the German aircraft were visible from the side windows of the house we were using near the village . . . I was sitting at my receiver and was lucky enough to be on their actual frequency at the time . . . I heard 'Sieg Heil! . . . Sieg Heil!' . . . and something about 'Bomben!', although I cannot remember all that was said, as my German was largely academic. But I could see the black crosses on the aircraft quite clearly and watched the bombs dropping from them."

Patrol Officer Fry, of the Folkestone Auxiliary Fire Service was ordered to the aerodrome with his section. The Auxiliaries were still a comparatively untried force, regarded by members of the regular fire brigade with a degree of tolerance and sometimes amusement.

When Fry arrived at Hawkinge a chaotic scene greeted him. He wrote,

". . . there were fires in many places and some seemed inaccessible . . . the huge water tower on stilts, supplying pressure for hydrants had been holed by flying bomb splinters. It reduced our mains supply to a mere trickle. We found a sunken static water tank close to a burning hangar but to reach it we had to remove sections of iron railings and cut down some small ornamental trees. But on top of the railings ran a number of thick electric cables."

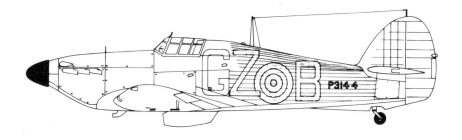

Hawker Hurricane Mk.1 32 Squadron Royal Air Force Biggin Hill and Hawkinge 1940

It was George Rumsey who found the cables, he shouted to Fry, "What shall I do with these?"

Fry replied, "Cut them!"

It was some hours later when a weary signalman found the severed cable ends. His rage was to be seen to be believed!

"What bloody fool cut communications to the guns?" he roared.

Fry and Rumsey looked at each other but somehow it was not the right moment for a confession!

Firemen were troubled by a constant series of small explosions and found the source was a small-arms store burning, where belts of ammunition were going off in the intense heat.

"Among the debris were a couple of Hurricanes," wrote Fry, ". . . but no attempt to salvage them could be made until morning. Our priority was to get the station operational as soon as possible."

The Watch Office, somehow, had remained unscathed throughout the raid and, although telephone communication with the outside world was non-existent, wireless contact with aircraft was still possible. Mike Crossley, leading No. 32 Squadron back to Hawkinge, looked down on the devastation below and asked for permission to land. There were a few anxious minutes spent by airmen and gunners who watched the Hurricanes gently make their landings on the bomb-cratered field. At that time no one knew if unexploded bombs were out on the field!

Throughout the night, supplied with gallons of tea and sandwiches from a mobile canteen, the airmen and firemen toiled amongst the debris and, when at long last dawn broke, they were heartened to see three Hurricanes take off to patrol the aerodrome.

"We felt like cheering," wrote Fry, ". . . but we were too tired!"

Later that morning, as they made their way back to Folkestone, and a late breakfast, they had that unmistakable feeling that, at last, they had become firemen!

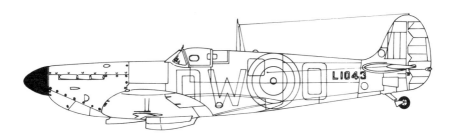

Supermarine Spitfire Mk.1 610 (County of Chester) Squadron Royal Auxiliary Air Force.
Biggin Hill, Gravesend & Hawkinge 1940

Within three days the aerodrome was to receive its second air raid, on Thursday 15th, which began as a fine sunny day. It had been an extraordinarily quiet morning despite the troops, sent up from Shorncliffe Camp, who were out on the airfield filling-in the craters.

At the dispersals the Hurricanes of No. 501 Squadron stood at 'readiness', while on the other side of the English Channel, near Calais, over one hundred German aircraft were assembling. Of the sixty or so JU87 Stuka dive-bombers now approaching our coast, one half peeled off towards Lympne, while the remainder set course towards Hawkinge.

The telephone in the Watch Office rang. The Hurricanes scrambled. As ground-crew watched the fighters climb away a whistle blew and a voice shouted over the Tannoy loudspeakers 'RUN! . . . RUN!' There was a sudden crash of gunfire which burst upon the ears of running airmen and soldiers. Above them, peeling into their dives, were the gull-winged dive-bombers. Their snarling engines and the screaming device which had put terror into the hearts of the Warsaw citizens, merged with the thunder of exploding bombs. Everywhere seemed to be alive with hot shrapnel and whining bullets. The sergeants' barrack block erupted in smoke and flames. No. 5 hangar disappeared – blasted into rubble.

On the occasion of the second raid, Marion McNeill, the WAAF, was caught out in the open while walking towards the aerodrome. She wrote:

". . . I looked up and there were the Stukas approaching . . . I stopped, and watched fascinated by the graceful curves they made before diving . . . the screaming they made was nerve shattering. Standing on sentry-duty at a road block near the cemetary gates, was a poor Army boy. I grabbed him and together we fell headlong into bushes nearby . . . something exploded near us . . . suddenly we were being covered with earth and decanted foul-smelling pond water!"

When the raid had subsided Marion asked where the nearest shelter was and, when she reached it, she found about fifteen young boys in uniform crowded together at one end.

"Their faces," Marion recalled, ". . . were literally green!" She added, ". . . my own nervousness seemed to diappear in a flash!"

Of the seven Stukas shot down, Sgt. Lawrence got two before he was shot down into the sea off Folkestone. Another was sent down in flames by Sgt. Farnes, and Sgt. McKay got a fourth. Both Flt. Lt. Putt and Gibson lost their Hurricanes over Folkestone. One of the crashing Stukas, brought down by the combination of many guns, smashed into electricity cables and partly demolished a house in Cheriton.

That particular crash site was visited by Fry, the Auxiliary fireman and his section.

"The body of the pilot lay decapitated in the front garden," Fry remembered, ". . . one of my crew found his pay-book . . . he was a young man who had held pilot rank only nine days. Another member of my crew found an unexploded 500lb bomb, which had catapulted into one of the bedrooms . . . we removed ourselves smartly!"

Further damage had been sustained by the aerodrome and by mid-afternoon the sky became filled with German bombers of all descriptions. No. 32 Squadron, who had been at 'readiness' at Hawkinge, were scrambled to intercept the enemy over Harwich. It was fortunate for the raiders of KG1 and KG2, who swept in over the airfield, completely unannounced, and who dropped their bombs and fled before the gunners knew what was happening. Damage was, fortunately, only slight and there were few casualties.

On August 28th, the radar screens near Dover, saw the build-up of enemy activity in the Pas de Calais and, by 0.900 hrs, Dorniers, Heinkels and Messerschmitts began passing over the Kent coasts. Fighter Command sent up three fighter squadrons who scattered the raiders near Rochford and Eastchurch. But the sixty or so escorting fighters, the Messerschmitt 109's, were not so easily discouraged. Dog-fights ensued over the whole of Kent. Of the fifteen or so German fighters shot down on that day, three were to go down under the guns of No. 501 Squadron, and all were within a five mile radius of Folkestone.

One of them was to hurtle into the ground at Selstead, just two miles from the aerodrome, observed by Arthur Edney, a local farmer.

Arthur had stood beside his horse and cart, surveying the air battles in progress in the clear morning sunlight, and half expecting Hitler's invasion that everyone was talking about. The sky was filled with the sounds of war. Spent cartridges and bits of aircraft whistled into trees and hedgerows, causing strutting partridge to take flight.

Arthur remembered that morning as if it was yesterday.

"I heard this strange screaming noise getting louder and louder . . . when I looked up I could see just a whirling blur coming straight towards us. I took hold of the halter because the horse got restless . . . then — no more than about thirty yards away at the most . . . with a terrific bang . . . the blur disappeared over a hedge into a nearby field."

126

Arthur went into the next field and peered over the crater's edge to see a tangled mass of twisted metal and burnt electrical harness. As he stood back, shielding his eyes from the bright sunlight, he saw the pilot, Oberleutnant Erich Kircheis, dangling from his parachute, slowly descending towards the village of Denton.

On the following day another German pilot, Oberleutnant Floorke, baled out of his stricken fighter in sight of the aerodrome, when sergeant Lacey of No. 501 Squadron shot Floorke's Messerschmitt to pieces. That was also the occasion when the aerodrome's gunners became frustrated by the sheer weight of RAF fighters. Bofors guns traversed this way and that in the hope of finding a target, but our fighters seemed to be everywhere.

On September 1st, Hawkinge received another raid in the late afternoon when a section of 'Zestorer' Bf 110 fighter-bombers suddenly sprang out of the Alkham Valley, without warning. They shot over the perimeter fences before the guns could open fire. An Observer Corps post near Capel was making a telephone call to the aerodrome to warn of a possible attack, when the fighter-bombers returned from the opposite direction. With the sun behind them they made small targets as they dived to drop their 250lb bombs amongst the station buildings.

And so the battles raged on. Every day brought new traumatic experiences to test Fighter Command personnel. Pilots were fighting gallantly while ground crews were nursing ailing aircraft. They worked as a team — men and machines — flesh and steel.

The designers of the aerodrome mortuary could never have envisaged or even contemplated such numbers killed, for the tiny building measured only 12 feet square!

There were of course many who never reached that little mortuary. One was Pilot Officer Keith Gillman, who had learned to fly with the Cambridge University Squadron before the war. At the age of nineteen he was flying Hurricanes, and during the summer battles of 1940, with No. 32 Squadron, it became important to him that he was especially able to defend his own home town of Dover. Fatigue probably had impaired his reflexes when a German fighter found him near St. Margaret's Bay, escorting a Blenheim engaged on radar re-calibration. Keith was never seen alive again, but ironically, his smiling face was to adorn national press advertisements, picture magazines, War Office posters and street hoardings, for weeks afterwards, during a recruiting campaign.

Probably one of the most remarkable events to occur at RAF Hawkinge, during the Battle of Britain, was the occasion when a German pilot decided to make a visit.

It was on Friday September 6th, when Kesselring had sent off a massive formation of bombers escorted by the indomitable Messerschmitts. Feldwebel Werner Gottschalk, piloting his Bf109 fighter, had taken off from the forward German airfield at Desvres, France, and set course with others of his unit for the Thames Estuary.

Nearing Chatham, anti-aircraft shells plastered the evening sky. It was such an

A wooden mock-up of a Hurricane fighter used for sequences in the 'Battle of Britain' film

One of several static non-flying Spitfires seen at RAF Hawkinge in the summer of 1968, during the filming of the 'Battle of Britain'

intense barrage that the German bombers released their bombs and broke formation. Flying high above them Gottschalk kept a watchful eye for the expected RAF fighters, but a shell found its mark. His machine spun over onto its back and dived out of control. At a considerable height disadvantage the German pilot found he was heading towards the English coast. Near Canterbury a British fighter got onto his tail but only made a passing attack. Nevertheless, it had been enough to stop his engine. Baling out over the English Channel was an indignity Gottschalk would avoid at all costs. It was then, in a mood of desperate optimism, that he spotted Hawkinge aerodrome.

Apprehensive, he approached the airfield with his wheels and flaps extended and locked. Making a landing with a Messerschmitt 109, even with a perfectly serviced engine, was always a difficulty. With no engine at all he prayed for his deliverance! The little fighter with only slight buffeting, landed on the grass beside No. 1 hangar and rolled to a stop. Gottschalk climbed out of the cockpit. It was only then that someone saw black crosses on the fuselage and wings. Amidst a fusillade of small-arms fire the German ran to the safety of the hangar where he was caught by a soldier.

A couple of months later another German fighter pilot was not so fortunate in his bid to escape from the coast.

It was coming up to 17.00 hrs when Staffel Kapitan Oberleutnant Vogt glanced at his wristwatch. Six minutes earlier the Udet IV Staffel, Jagdeschwader, one of two famous Luftwaffe fighter units, had dived groundwards from 20,000 feet just south of London. Vogt recognised the familiar coastline ahead when the tall radar masts at Dover appeared on his left. In another few seconds the green countryside would drop away sharply from the North Downs, above Folkestone, to reveal the English Channel. It was a familiar route — he had flown it many times before.

But vigilant anti-aircraft gunners, on 'Red Alert', were soon aware of impending action as the evening sky became pock-marked with shell smudges. In complete contrast to the large calibre A.A. guns on the cliffs, a lone Bofors gun was sited at the extreme end of the jutting, dog-leg pier at Folkestone. The crew had already reached their respective positions on the gun with alacrity. They were well disciplined and eager, but by no means successful. Until now they had never hit anything at all!

A Bombardier pressed an eye to the rubber sight flange. Then the whole gun platform traversed as he turned handles until an incredibly fast blur filled his vision.

"ON! . . . ON! . . . ON! . . . " he shouted. The firing plate was depressed and the barrel recoiled as each charge detonated. 'Taffy' Jones followed the blur, his tin helmet biting into the nape of his neck. Then he shouted, "Got him! . . . got the bastard!"

Vogt felt his machine lurch drunkenly as if pushed by an unseen hand. Oil and coolant spattered across the windshield, and a strong smell of cordite invaded the confines of the cockpit.

The German War-Grave section at the Hawkinge cemetery

The only remaining Picket Hamilton Fort still in existence on the airfield at Hawkinge

Elated with their new-found success the Bofors crew watched the crippled fighter skimming the sea, hopping and skipping from wave top to wave top, like a flat stone hurled across a still lake, until it stopped about fifty yards from the shore.

Releasing the hood-catches, Vogt punched open the perspex canopy. The inrush of hot pungent engine fumes was sickening. He undid the harness and slid into the water.

Police Constable Williams remembers that event.

"Inspector Bill Ffloyd, and myself," P.C. Williams told me, ". . . were on our way down the cliff path towards where the German pilot had come ashore . . . I can see the pilot now— flinching and drawing back when I elbowed my way through a group of soldiers. I remember shouting at him, 'You Nazi bastard!. . . shooting innocent women and children!' " Williams had lost his temper because only a day or so previous he had seen a young child killed by a German fighter straffing the town.

However, it is strange to record that Vogt and Williams became quite friendly whilst the pilot was being documented at the Folkestone Police Station later. It was during that time at the station that Vogt had said, "Perhaps — if we both survive this war you will visit me and my family. I would be honoured!" P.C. Cyril Ashley Williams, a member of the old Folkestone Borough Police Force since 1934, shook the pilot's hand and said in reply,

"Goodbye . . . the war is over for you my lad — but take care — I might just take you up on your offer one day!"

The Battle of Britain drew to a close towards the end of 1940, and the Blitz on London and other major cities was a new phase in German tactics. There are, however, many eminent historians who believe that epic battle continued into 1941, and not without some evidence have they reached their theories.

Although the German war machine had received one set-back after another, putting back time and again the proposed invasion of the British Isles, the Luftwaffe maintained a series of air attacks by day and night. But with renewed strength the Royal Air Force began intruder operations over enemy-held France, Belgium and Holland. The South-East aerodromes, most of which had received their fair share of aerial bombardment, were now the 'jump-off' airfields for these intruder missions. It was now the turn of the RAF to blast the German forward airfields, fuel dumps, harbour installations, railways, roads and bridges of communication.

In 1941 Hawkinge gained its own squadron of Spitfires when a small flight of them was given squadron status. The new squadron, No. 91 (Nigerian), was a special unit operating reconnaissance sorties, and was actually performing 'Jim Crow' duties initially flown by the previous No. 421 Flight. Although the squadron's prime purpose was reconnaissance, reporting on enemy shipping movements and Luftwaffe formations, the pilots never failed to seize the opportunity of attacking isolated ships, gun emplacements, airfields and individual aircraft. The unit gained many kills, lost some very good pilots and a large

A sound detector bowl situated on the North Downs above the town of Hythe, Kent (Author)

Hawkinge 1980. Closed by the RAF in 1959, the site is in private hands. Interestingly enough, the airfield saw a bustle of activity in the 1960's as much of the film 'Battle of Britain' was made there.   (Len Pilkington)

proportion were decorated. Squadron personalities included 'Moses' Demozay, Maridor and Demoline, all Frenchmen; Le Roux of South Africa; Spurdle and Pannell of New Zealand, Donahue and Young from the United States of America.

It was not until June 1941 that a couple of Lysander aircraft arrived at Hawkinge to form No. 277 Air Sea Rescue Squadron. There are many references in official records to the gallantry of the squadron's personnel who, using the Lysander and later the Walrus amphibian, snatched drowning airmen from the sea. For three years that particular squadron maintained a unique service at the aerodrome unequalled in any theatre of the Second World War.

Towards the end of the war Hawkinge played host to many fighter squadrons of different nationalities; Czech, Dutch, Belgian, Canadian and Australian, until finally hostilities ceased in 1945.

Of all the aircraft types to grace the aerodrome with their presence the Spitfire, that graceful fighter which became a legend in its own right, remained dominant throughout. But soon the Jet-age was upon us and the inevitable happened. This small grass airfield, lacking modern runways and unsuitable for high-powered, sophisticated aircraft, became obsolete practically overnight.

And so two years after hostilities had ceased the aerodrome had changed completely from a thriving fighter station to a home for the Womens Auxiliary Air Force Technical Training Depot. The Womens Royal Air Force, as they later became known, were still operating there when the aerodrome closed down.

Now, when one looks back over the aerodrome's long history, when fighter squadrons arrived to be cared for, their aircraft serviced and pilots revered and respected for individual gallantry, you can still hear the boisterousness of such dedicated young men in the empty corridors of decaying buildings.

Royal Air Force Hawkinge achieved immortal fame and earned the gratitude of a nation through a combination of strategic locality, some pilot infallibility and the tenacity of ordinary men.

Michael Crossley wrote a fitting epitaph in one of his letters,

". . . good old Hawkinge provided plenty to talk about. You could watch the Messerschmitts pooping-off the Dover balloon barrage first thing in the morning. . . or watch a totally unannounced stick of bombs drop across the 'drome. But they never did it any lasting harm. It gives me a hell of a lump in the throat when I see those lovely RAF stations decaying . . . especially if you knew them in peace-time before the war as I did."

"Dear Hawkinge . . . I have never been back . . . but I'll remember it . . . in very sharp focus!"

Indeed we will.

GB 1089 bc
Maßstab etwa 1: 9800
(1cm,: 98 m)
1km
500
0

Gravesend
Flugplatz

G.B.1089 bc
N.f.D.

Kriegsaufnahme
029
Nachträge:
8.11.40

Karte:
1:100 000
Blatt 34

Länge
(ostw. Greenw.):
0°24'
Nördl. Breite:
51°25'

Zielhöhe
über N N 73 m

G.B. 1089 Flugplatz

1. Flugzeughallen
2. Werft
3. Nebengebäude
4. Scheinwerfer- oder Horchgerät-Stellung
5. Fla-M.G.-Stellung

Lfl. Kdo. 2, Nov. 1940

Gravesend 8.11.1940. Note aircraft at dispersal around airfield.   (Christopher R. Elliott)

134

R.A.F. GRAVESEND DURING THE
BATTLE OF BRITAIN

By C. R. Munday

July 1940 saw RAF Gravesend as a satellite station of Biggin Hill. It was a civilian airport with a bumpy grass surface which had been requisitioned by the Air Ministry upon the outbreak of war in September 1939. The control tower and clubhouse was used for most of the functions of the airfield except for the work carried out on the aircraft. This was done in the three hangars. In one of the hangars was the famous DH88 racing aircraft G-ACSS winner of the 1934 MacRobertson Air Race to Australia. Also on the airfield was a small factory where Essex Aero manufactured fuel tanks for Spitfires and other aircraft.

Squadrons were rotated from Biggin Hill for duty at Gravesend. Their numbers had been swelled earlier in the year when other squadrons of aircraft had been drafted in, temporarily, to cover the evacuation of the Allied forces from France. After this had been achieved, activities had lulled for a short time, but it was to be the lull before the storm.

On 3rd July 1940, instead of a day fighter squadron from Biggin Hill, 604 (County of Middlesex) Squadron arrived from Northolt. They were flying twin-engined Bristol Blenheim IF aircraft which had been fitted with a gun pack under the fuselage and were intended to be used as a stop-gap night fighter. At this time the early airborne radar sets were being tested and 604 Squadron took part in these trials. It was necessary to use a fairly large aircraft to carry the equipment and crew of pilot and radar operator.

Night fighter patrols took place on most nights without any contact being made with enemy aircraft. Searchlight co-operation flights also took place on several occasions, whilst on 19th airfiring practice took place at Leysdown bombing and gunnery range on the nearby Isle of Sheppey. As the month wore on, the forthcoming battle was entering its first phase and the decision was taken to move 604 Squadron to Middle Wallop to make way for a further squadron of day fighters at Gravesend. The move took place on 26th when a Bristol Bombay aircraft moved some of the personnel, whilst the others left in the Blenheims or by train from Gravesend Station.

On the same day 501 (County of Gloucester) Squadron moved into Gravesend and immediately entered the daytime fighting. This squadron was a pre-war auxiliary unit with many pilots being of sergeant rank. They flew Hawker Hurricane Mark I fighters and had been the first auxiliary squadron to be equipped with this aircraft. The officers of the squadron used the aero-club accommodation in the control tower whilst the sergeants slept in an empty house in Thong Lane which ran alongside the aerodrome. Meals were eaten in a hut behind one of the hangars.

Control tower and clubhouse at Gravesend used by pilots of 501 and 66 Squadrons during Battle of Britain (R. Munday)

Gravesend in wartime camouflage photographed in the 1950's (Christopher R. Elliott)

One of the sergeant pilots was J.H. (Ginger) Lacey, then a young unknown pilot later destined to become famous as an air ace. In his book "Ginger Lacey — Fighter Pilot", R.T. Bickers tells how on 30th August a newsreel camera crew took film of the squadron taking off for battle and being delighted when Lacey returned and glided in to make a forced landing. They thought it had been enacted for their cameras, but bullets from a German aircraft had caused his engine to seize up. When Sgt. Lacey went home to Yorkshire on leave on 7th September he had shot down 15 enemy aircraft, and had been awarded the DFM.

Whilst 501 Squadron was at Gravesend they used the regular RAF fighter aerodrome at Hawkinge as their forward base. This enabled standing patrols to be carried out for as long as possible and aircraft would refuel and rearm without the need to return to Gravesend during the day. Each evening the squadron would return for a snatched rest before the next day's patrols and dogfights.

On 26th July Flt/Lt. Cox was shot down in mistake by the anti-aircraft guns at Dover whilst 501's Hurricanes tangled with Messerschmitt Bf109 fighters. On 29th a formation of Junkers JU87 dive bombers, escorted by Bf109's, was intercepted and six aircraft were claimed as destroyed. The next day continued fine and clear and after patrolling over the Dover area during the day, P/O Don was injured when he had to take to his parachute. On arrival at Gravesend P/O Parkin undershot the aerodrome when landing and was seriously injured.

Over the next few days 501 continued to patrol above the Kentish coast without much action, so on 4th August they carried out air-to-air firing practice at the Holbeach range in Lincolnshire. On 5th and 6th patrols were mounted over Deal and Dover without being called into action. On 7th, the squadron arrived at Hawkinge at 5.30 a.m. but returned to Gravesend at 8.40 a.m. The weather was bad, and two Hurricanes of yellow section were wrecked when they collided whilst landing. Neither pilot suffered injury. Although the day continued overcast numerous patrols were mounted but no interceptions took place. On 9th the weather was again overcast and red section stayed overnight at Hawkinge. They were joined on 10th at 5.30 a.m. by the remainder of the squadron and an interception of a German bomber was foiled when it escaped in cloud. On the 12th a large force of JU87's was intercepted, and several were destroyed. P/O Lukaszewicz was shot down and killed in this action. In the afternoon a further large force of German aircraft was encountered west of Ramsgate, the squadron returning to Gravesend in the early evening. On the next two days 501 flew from Gravesend without landing at Hawkinge as their forward base had been badly damaged by bombing. On 15th and 16th further interceptions of large forces took place, but the 17th proved a quiet day for 501. The 18th was a particularly busy day with dogfights taking place over most of Southern Kent. The squadron lost F/Lt. Stoney and P/O Bland, both killed on this day. Several other pilots were injured. Deterioration of the weather prevented successful interceptions on the next few days. On 24th, thirty Junkers JU88 bombers were attacked after they had dropped their bombs on Manston aerodrome. P/O Zenker was killed on this day. Sgt. Glowaki managed to shoot

ACI Donald V. Elliott at Cobham Hall October 1940 — Author of letters from 66 (F) Squadron at Gravesend during Battle of Britain   (C.R. Elliott)

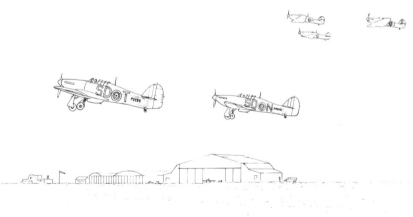

Hurricanes of 501 (County of Gloucester) Squadron scramble from Gravesend.

down an escorting Bf109 whilst P/O Aldridge broke an arm after baling out of his crashing Hurricane. Two of the JU88's were claimed as destroyed. Again, on 25th and 26th, no interceptions took place whilst on 27th, the weather was fine and clear with the Hurricanes of 501 again in the thick of the battle. The squadron C.O., S/Ldr. Hogan, was forced to land with a leaking glycol coolant tank after his aircraft was hit whilst attacking a Dornier Do215 bomber. In the late afternoon, when the squadron had returned to Gravesend they were visited by the father of the RAF, Air Chief Marshal Viscount Trenchard, who had returned to active duty in order to help boost morale.

On 28th, a fine clear day saw 501 engage a force of 17 bombers escorted by Bf109 fighters. During the action three of the escort were claimed shot down. The next day 501 did not encounter the enemy until early evening when they were pounced on by a force of nine Bf109's, who attacked out of the sun. F/Lt. Gibson and Sgt. Green were forced to bale out of their aircraft and parachute to safety. Sgt. Lacey claimed a Bf109 as destroyed. The next day the squadron engaged large forces of German aircraft several times during the day in attempts to break up the formations before they could reach their targets. Several of the enemy were claimed as destroyed, whilst Sgt. Lacey was forced down with a damaged radiator. It was on this day that heavy bombing destroyed the communication centre at Biggin Hill, the sector station. Whilst Biggin Hill was out of action, Hornchurch, just across the River Thames, took control of 501's aircraft. On the last day of August, seven Hurricanes took off from Gravesend at 1 p.m. to engage a fighter escort over Gravesend, and three aircraft were claimed as destroyed. Sgt. Glowaki baled out of his burning aircraft and was slightly injured. September opened with an interception over Tunbridge Wells on the 1st. The next day, just before 8 a.m., bombs were dropped on the edge of Gravesend airfield but no damage was caused, although two soldiers were slightly injured. The Hurricanes had taken off shortly before, but were unable to prevent the bombs being dropped. In this action, and another later in the day, 501 suffered casualties when P/O Rose Price was killed; it was his first day with the squadron. Sgt. Henn and P/O Skalski being injured. Bombs were again dropped near Gravesend airfield on 4th. P/O Skalski was again injured on 5th when heavy fighting took place over Maidstone. A large formation of German aircraft was attacked over Ashford on the next day and 501 lost two pilots: Sgts. Adams and Houghton who were both killed. The squadron records state that on the 7th they intercepted the largest formations they had ever met; four large waves of bombers escorted by both Bf109 and the twin engined Messerschmitt Bf110's. The next three days saw 501 carrying out patrols, but with only limited interceptions being reported. On the 10th they were instructed to move to Kenley in Surrey. In turn a regular Spitfire squadron moved from Kenley to Gravesend. This was 66 Squadron which had been the very first squadron to receive Spitfire fighter aircraft, introduced some two years previously. Commanded by Sqd/Ldr. R. Leigh they had been in the thick of the fighting whilst at Kenley. They continued to use Hawkinge as their forward base, as 501 had done. On most days

Site of old Gravesend Airport January 1979. Part of old perimeter track in top lefthand corner
(Len Pilkington)

they flew interception patrols, making regular contact with the enemy, but as the weather deteriorated so the pace of the battle decreased. On October 30th, 66 Squadron was posted to nearby West Malling. Earlier in October, 421 Flight had been formed at Gravesend on Winston Churchill's instigation. This flight flew Spitfires for a short while but these were replaced by Hurricane IIa's for the rest of the time the flight spent at Gravesend. Their duty was to fly high over the German Luftwaffe assembly points on the coast of the continent and radio back information on the numbers of aircraft and the direction of heading.

Whilst 66 Squadron and 421 Flight were at Gravesend a young regular airman sent home letters to his family in Suffolk. Aircraftsman Grade I Donald Elliott was an engine fitter who had been trained at Halton as an RAF apprentice before the war. His letters have been preserved by his brother and record the scene at Gravesend through the words of a member of the squadron, fighting through the battle, whilst working on the ground. Several pilots of the squadron have since recorded in print their experiences of these days, but AC1 Elliott's letters are probably unique. Donald Elliott came to Gravesend as a member of 66 Squadron but was transferred to 421 Flight on its formation, although he continued to work alongside his old colleagues of 66 Squadron.

On 18th September he writes, "The few of us in maintenance flight are billeted away from the aerodrome. The first two nights we had here we lived in a pretty cafe in some woods. It was built of wood and glass and stood on piles over a lake. We had rowing boats on the lake and there were thousands of fish, so you can imagine what it was like. It was called Laughing Waters" (since rebuilt as the Inn on the Lake). "Now we have moved to a huge hall built round about the year 1589, it's called Cobham Hall" — the letter continues, "It's like being on a battlefield here, there are dozens of huge naval and anti-aircraft guns all round here and every night they fire hundreds of rounds an hour, it's a constant barrage to keep machines off London. They also fire during the day whilst 'Jerry' is over. There were plenty over this morning so we didn't get much peace. It rains shrapnel night and day, so we have to wear tin hats outside. Nine German bombers came over here on Wednesday afternoon and they wouldn't break the formation. I counted 250 shell bursts in the sky in about three minutes and I didn't go on counting then. One bomber was shot down, you should have heard the noise when he hit the ground and his bombs went up.

"I expect you read about the huge fires started along the Thames. Well we saw those. The one of the Surrey Docks burnt for days and nights. We can see down over the Thames from the aerodrome as we are on top of a hill and on the sides (of the Thames) are these big oil storage tanks. They have been empty since war started and they have just finished filling them up a few days ago. 'Jerry' was over the same night and set them on fire, he tried again for some more this morning only he missed!."

Later, in September, AC1 Elliott records his feelings whilst on fire duties after his normal daytime duties. "I am up in the hangar writing this as I have to stand by the fire tender from half past six tonight until the same time tomorrow.

I shall be working tomorrow just the same . . ." "If there's no raid warnings in the camp I won't have to got out of here again tonight. I won't be sorry because the wind is blowing a gale and it's pouring with rain. For the last night or two it's been bright moonlight and there have been dozens of enemy aircraft over. Last night they dropped a few round the camp but they did no damage as they fell in the fields . . ." "It's a wonderful sight to see sixty or eighty huge German bombers flying in formation towards London through a barrage of hundreds and hundreds of anti-aircraft shells. They generally have to turn back or on to another course. We got 5 machines in yesterday's fighting. One of our boys has not come back, he went down over the sea off Dover. On the Sunday (15th) when the total was 185 we got 16 of them without a single loss." Post war research brings the figure of 185 down to about 60 aircraft but confused reports of several RAF pilots claiming the same aircraft shot down lead to these false figures. Again AC1 Elliott writes home, "I was going to write this on Sunday as it was our day off but during the morning we were called back to work as we get no days off again so I didn't have a chance to write then. I expect you saw the late news on Monday morning when the Germans claimed that Gravesend and Tilbury were in flames didn't you, well from here we can see every part of them both and the only smoke you can see is from the factories. Anti aircraft shot down a German fighter over here yesterday. Well there's plenty of work to be done today as two of our machines ran into each other yesterday. That's where your Spitfire fund goes to!" This last reference is to the many funds set up by towns, works and organisations to provide money for the construction of further Spitfires.

In late October he writes, "It's been raining here all day and still is. Jerry has been over nevertheless. Tonight he dropped 2 (bombs) on the civilian houses on the far side of the 'drome. We got no warning."

Writing home on 27th October to tell his parents that he would be moving to another aerodrome soon, he inserts a small drawing of a Nissen hut in his letter, "I am not at Cobham Hall any longer but in a hut on the far side of the 'drome . . . It's alright only there are no lights, so anything we want to do at night we have to use a torch or candles. 'Jerry' came over the other afternoon (23rd) about 4.30 and dropped three just off the 'drome. One scored a direct hit on a row of lovely houses. There's not a bit of one left, just a big hole and the house each side is nearly down. Four were killed, and two injured. The next day we had eleven time bombs go off in the fields around the aerodrome." Donald Elliott finished his letters from Gravesend by asking his parents to excuse his writing as his hands were cold and he had been up since 6 a.m. Soon after he became a Leading Aircraftman and was posted to the Far East. He continued to record his experiences after he was taken prisoner of war by the Japanese. He died on 17th March 1945 in North Borneo.

Whilst at Gravesend 66 Squadron lost five pilots killed, and 421 flight, one pilot. All the pilots (except one, F/Lt. Cox) killed during the Battle of Britain whilst flying from Gravesend, are now commemorated on a memorial plaque affixed to the wall of Thong Lane Sports Centre built on part of the wartime extensions to the aerodrome.

Chapter Eight

WEST MALLING

By Robin J. Brooks

West Malling began life as a civil flying club in 1930 bearing the name of Maidstone Airport. It was just a field with a collection of huts, together with a clubhouse in one corner, and often known as Kingshill. At the time it was used for gliding, but this was not its only use. A company calling itself Kent Aeronautical Services operated from the field using such aircraft as modified SE.5A's called Dudley Watt DW1's and a Sopwith Dove G-EBKY which was owned by C. H. Lowe-Wylde. This was abandoned at the airfield after the owner's death in a powered glider that he had designed and built himself and survives today at the Shuttleworth Collection.

Maidstone Airport was registered as a company on 25th July, 1932. In December the same source records that in the aerodrome directory of Great Britain and Northern Ireland, Maidstone (West Malling) was a civil aerodrome five miles west of Maidstone and one mile from West Malling town.

In 1935 Malling Aviation became the proprietors of the airfield and renamed it Malling Aero Club, West Malling Aerodrome, Kent. So the field changed names and the title of Maidstone Airport was left to history.

With the expansion of the Royal Air Force during 1937/8, West Malling came under the wing of the Director of Works, Air Ministry. More land was acquired, the field began to grow and the workmen arrived to build more permanent buildings and put West Malling onto a war footing.

The aerodrome is set upon one of the highest ridges in Kent. Climbing from the village of Malling with the airfield on your left side, the road reaches the top of the ridge to drop down the other side into a village called Mereworth. The field is perched on the top of the ridge.

Looking at the history of the Royal Air Force in the second world war, it does not tell us much about West Malling in the opening stages of 1939. What it does say is that the station was out of action for some considerable time during 1940, due to enemy action.

From the records we read that on July 12th 1940, 141 Squadron arrived at West Malling with the Boulton Paul Defiant, a two seater fighter. This squadron joined No. 26 Army Co-operation Squadron flying the Lysander.

On July 25th 141 saw action when they engaged the enemy over a convoy in mid-channel. Flying Messerschmitt 110's, the Germans attacked the Defiants flying from the direction of the sun. They had realised that the Defiant was very vulnerable when attacked from below. The turret did not move sufficiently for the gunner to fire down on the enemy. The squadron was badly hit, only one returning to Malling. The remainder of the personnel and aircraft were posted

The Focke-Wulf 190 of Otto Bechtold
landed at Malling in error 17th April
1943. Pictured in front of Malling
Control Tower (Imperial War Museum)

Drawing of aircraft flown at West Malling
1943, by unknown artist

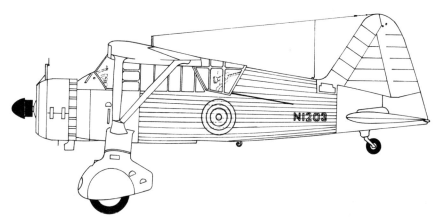

Westland Lysander Mk.II 26 Army Co-operation Squadron West Malling 1939-40

forthwith to Prestwick from where they had come. This, and similar incidents, caused the Defiant to be retired prematurely from the front line.

With the departure of 141 Squadron, Malling was left with just 26 Squadron. On August 10th, the Luftwaffe began a series of attacks that rendered the airfield unserviceable for most of the Battle.

At 07.30 on the morning of Saturday the 10th a Dornier 17 of Kampfgeschwader 2 stalked in over the coast near Deal and dropped its load of light bombs in the vicinity of the airfield. No warning of attack was given, as the aeroplane emerged from heavy cloud carrying out two runs; entering the cloud between each attack. The Dornier dropped fourteen bombs on the airfield, some among the requisitioned premises of the new station, and some in the surrounding fields. Two aircraft of 26 Squadron were damaged by machine gun fire and flying splinters. Many windows in nearby buildings were shattered, and 17 workmen were also injured by flying splinters. Three Royal Engineer Sappers received minor injuries when one bomb fell on the building that they were occupying. The aircraft was attacked by the ground defence posts but no hits were recorded. The raid had only lasted about three minutes when the Dornier re-entered the heavy cloud. It did not return.

On Thursday August 15th a high altitude attack was made on West Malling. The target however should have been Biggin Hill. At 1900 hours a Dornier Gruppe appeared at the southern end of the airfield and commenced systematic bombing. Two airmen were killed, and considerable damage was done. The runways were badly straddled, leaving gaping craters in the grass. Several blister hangars were put out of use and one ambulance was written off. The station personnel were put to work in seeing that the airfield quickly returned to an operational level, and had nearly completed this task when, on 16th August, the Luftwaffe returned.

West Malling control tower   (Robin J. Brooks)

Main Gate of the airfield 1964   (Robin J. Brooks)

The enemy formation was tracked by radar to the North Foreland where it split into two formations. Two Staffeln of KG.2's Dorniers turned to approach Malling and the element of surprise was achieved. Repair teams were still in the process of clearing rubble and filling the craters when the raid swept in from the north east. More than eighty high-explosive and fragmentation bombs fell, destroying a Lysander and ensuring that the station remained out of action for four days.

Again on the 18th West Malling was subjected to a medium attack by Dornier 17's of 9/KG 76 and Junker's 88's of 11/KG 76. Further damage was sustained by the Lysanders of 26 Squadron and several hangars were hit. No casualties were reported but the local population began to curse the fact that the airfield existed within their midst.

This was the last of the big raids that hit Malling, though several lone raiders attacked the field from time to time. The worst single attack took place on September 10th. At 1720 hours, a single Dornier 17 made a run over the airfield and dropped six anti-personnel bombs. One bomb scored a direct hit on a post of Queen's Regiment soldiers killing six of them, and wounding another three. One airman was also injured by falling down a trench. Two buildings were gutted by fire, and the grass field was badly cratered. The bombs were dropped from about 5,000 feet.

Something to relieve the monotony of constant bombing took place on the 15th. A Heinkel 111 was forced to land on the airfield at 1500 hours. With eight or nine Hurricanes and Spitfires attacking it, it skimmed over the boundary of the field trailing smoke from its engines, touched down and rolled to a stop. The Intelligence Officer at West Malling managed to have a word with the pilot who seemed confident that his country would win. He was marched off to the guard room.

The story of what actually happened was told some time later. 238 Squadron, flying Hurricanes, and based at Middle Wallop, had attacked a formation of eighteen Heinkels as they returned from bombing London. They attacked in the vicinity of West Malling, with one Hurricane suffering an engine seizure. As it poured bullets into the Heinkel, the pilot saw Malling below. He came in for an emergency landing and, to his amazement, saw the Heinkel, which he had just attacked, also come in for an emergency landing. Running over to the Heinkel, the Hurricane pilot hoped to meet his opponent in battle, but the German pilot was already on his way to the guard room.

The bombing forced 26 Squadron to leave and it was not until 30th October 1940 that the station was ready to receive a full squadron, when 66 Squadron flew in with Spitfires. This unit had achieved a magnificent record during the Battle of Britain, flying from Coltishall in Norfolk and then from Kenley in Surrey. West Malling offered them a brief respite from the ordeal of constant battle. With 66 Squadron came 421 flight, undertaking fleet spotting duties and flying protection to the Fairey Swordfish squadrons based at Manston in Kent. Flying Hurricanes and Spitfires they faithfully acted as escorts to their slower charges.

West Malling 1979

(Len Pilkington)

West Malling had survived the Battle of Britain, it had been a hard fought battle but, for this one particular station the war had still some way to go. During 1941 a number of night fighter squadrons arrived. They flew a variety of aircraft including the somewhat vulnerable Defiant and the far more successful Beaufighter. For a time 1428 (enemy aircraft) Squadron was stationed there, allowing personnel to brush up their identification of Heinkels and Messerschmitts, whilst also allowing pilots to fly against these aircraft types.

On the night of April 16th 1943, came one of Malling's strangest incidents. A single engined aircraft was heard to be approaching the field. Thinking it to be a Defiant in trouble, many of the airmen came out to see what was happening. The aircraft circled twice, fired its colours of the day and proceeded to approach the airfield boundary. Having landed, the fire tender and crash crew went out to the aircraft to offer assistance. On approaching, the crash crew saw a large swastika on the side and a foreign language coming from a very agitated pilot. Reaching for their guns, the crash crew took the crestfallen pilot into custody. The aircraft was a Focke-wulf 190.

A minute later, another 190 was seen to approach and land. The beaverette rushed to the spot to head off the machine as the Nazi pilot realised his error and started to take off. Leading Aircraftman Sharlock gave a quick burst with the twin Vickers gun on the beaverette from 20 yards and saw a small fire in the cockpit, giving a second burst from the gun as the aircraft began to move along the runway. The pilot fell from the 190 and tried to run away. He was caught by several airmen and the station commander.

The oxygen bottles in the aircraft exploded and the whole aircraft disintegrated, pieces being thrown 300 yards away. Two fire tender airmen were seriously hurt as was the pilot of the 190. He was taken to the station sick-quarters and later to join the other German in the guard room. A third 190 under-shot the runway and landed in a cherry orchard at the lower end of the field, the pilot receiving a fractured skull. A fourth aircraft crashed at Staplehurst, the pilot being killed when his parachute failed to open in time. It was afterwards discovered that about fifteen Focke-wulf 190's came over on raids and, although equipped with long-range fuel tanks, ran out of fuel touching down when they thought they were back over occupied Europe. All of the aircraft had been covered in a sooty black type of paint as night camouflage.

In July 1943, West Malling began to accept heavy bombers of the Royal Air Force and the United States Air Force. Halifaxes, Lancasters, Fortresses and Liberators, often with many dead and wounded aboard, used the station as a take-off and landing base. The day squadrons were supplemented by Thunderbolts of the USAF, and often led by men who had flown over the fields of Kent before the Americans entered the war. Nos 234, 130 and 504 Squadrons were now based at Malling, flying as escorts to the ever increasing day-time bomber offensive.

With August 1943 approaching, day fighters began to arrive at the airfield for use as wings for long escorts to the bombers obeying Churchill's 'set Europe alight' speech. Flying in came 411, 485 and 610 Squadrons, all three being later used in combined operations for the Dieppe landing. 32 Squadron which had achieved fame during the Battle of Britain was also at Malling and saw Squadron Leader 'Johnnie' Johnson flying from the field.

On 12th June, 1944, the war and West Malling entered a new phase. 'Divers', the name given to pilotless aircraft, flew across the station, one landing in a field at Crouch near Borough Green. 91 Squadron became the main force to combat this new type of warfare, together with 274 who had just received the new Hawker Tempest. 157 Squadron arrived to supplement these two squadrons and established their officers' mess at Addington House just along the main road from the station. When the airmen discovered that the roadhouse on the Tonbridge to Sevenoaks road called the 'Hilden Manor' had a swimming pool within the grounds, this was immediately recruited for dinghy drill practise.

With these three squadrons, West Malling became the main base for tipping and destroying 'doodle bugs', and the night fighter squadrons moved out. On 18th June the three squadrons collectively shot down ten VI's, with one being seen to crash beyond the perimeter of the airfield. By 31st July, 278 flying bombs had been destroyed by West Malling aircraft and this achievement earned the station the title of main anti-doodlebug airfield.

The title was however short-lived for, in August, it was decided that the air-field would become a major base in peacetime. So war activities ceased at West Malling. From April 1941 until the premature close in August 1944, the station claimed to have been responsible for the destruction of 165 enemy aircraft together with 34 probably destroyed and 59 damaged. Big extensions would now be needed, together with a new concrete runway to allow the flying of the future jet aircraft. These major works were carried out between August 1944 and June 1945.

For a number of years RAF jets did fly from West Malling. Vampires, Meteors and eventually Javelins became a familiar sight. Yet, even with the major con-versions carried out at the end of the war, and again in the 1950s, the station was not secured from closure. In 1960 West Malling was placed under a care and maintenance unit, though a new lease of life was given to the station in the following year when it was used by a United States Navy facility flight. They remained there for two years before being transferred to Blackbushe. In their place came No. 618 gliding school and a servicing flight from Short Brothers, the aircraft manufacturers formerly based at Rochester. At this time they were engaged in government contracts for servicing and test flying RAF Chipmunks.

In 1970 the airfield was acquired by the Kent County Council to protect the site from undesirable development. Before this the site was a rehabilitation centre for the Ugandan Asians arriving in Britian.

The airfield and majority of buildings are in a very good state of preservation. Shorts have now left the field but the Council hope to re-open it for restricted commercial flying, despite a lot of local resistance.

From its origin as the Maidstone Flying Club to the present day, the station has earned a place in our history. Long may it remain a place of aviation.

Chapter Nine

ROCHESTER

By Philip MacDougall

During the summer of 1940, Rochester airfield was subjected to two major German air raids. This, though, is hardly surprising. As an airfield, Rochester was of considerable strategic value. In emergencies it could always be used by Fighter Command aircraft but, of even greater significance, was its worth to Bomber Command's war effort. Rochester airfield was the home of Short Brothers whose factory there, during that summer, was busily engaged in the production of Stirling bombers.

Rochester airfield dates back to 1933. At that time Rochester Corporation, co-operating with Short Brothers, decided that a municipal airport would bring certain advantages. Soon after the opening of the airfield Pobjoys, virtually a subsidiary of Shorts, established a factory there. Later, in 1938, the airfield also gained an RAF connection when No. 23 Elementary and Reserve Flying Training School was formed at Rochester. Among the aircraft in use were Hawker Harts, Avro Tutors and Miles Magisters. No. 23 Flying Training School, however, did not remain at Rochester for the war, being transferred to Belfast in September 1939.

As a civilian airfield, the Germans had been given ample opportunity to familiarize themselves with its layout. Prior to the outbreak of war, a number of Lufthansa aircraft over flew Rochester during flights to London. It can most certainly be assumed that they were taking photographs. One such aerial photograph, dated June 1939, was captured at the end of the war and shows considerable detail of the factory area.

A particular feature of the airfield which must have interested the Germans was the extensive additions then being made to this factory area. At the time, Shorts were preparing to build the new Stirling bomber and, to do so, constructed a completely new factory complex replete with hangars. Subsequently, when the first Stirling prototype was rolled out during the spring of 1939, the number of over flights by German 'civilian' aircraft grew measurably.

That year was also the one in which the airfield prepared for war. Large air raid shelters, very deep and lined with concrete, were built both around the airfield and close to the factory site. Later, in 1940, emplacements for anti-aircraft guns were prepared, whilst numerous slit trenches were dug. John Chinery, who was employed upon production work within the Stirling factory, vividly recalls the weeks leading up to and including the Battle of Britain. For him, never-to-be-forgotten sights became daily events. There were overhead battles, in which a Bf 109, hotly pursued by a cannon firing Spitfire, flew very low, hedge hopping, in a frantic attempt to escape. A Spitfire, minus one wing,

Rochester's Aerodrome 1935. The Pobjoy works can be seen in the foreground with Short Bros erection hangar on the left. ('Flight' photo)

Half scale Stirling (Short Bros)

The German objective in attacking Rocnester was to destroy production of the Stirling bomber. The second prototype is seen here at Rochester airport.   (Short Bros.)

spiralling down to crash in the Medway valley at Strood. A German fighter air-craft crashing in flames, the pilot plummeting to earth suspended under a faulty partially opened parachute, to terminate his young life for the Fatherland in the Davis Housing Estate close to Rochester airfield.

John Chinery's bus ride in the mornings from Frindsbury to the airport meant a change at Star Hill. During one such morning a blazing Dornier bomber descen-ded over the City, along the route of the River Medway, to crash on the Hoo Peninsula. At the 'all clear' the bus proceeded up Delce Road and, upon reaching St. William's Hospital, it was found that a bomb had exploded in front of the Hospital gate — segment of bomb casing, still hot, lay nearby on the road surface.

The night time defence procedure at the airfield was to plant a forest of wooden scaffold type poles scattered throughout the airfield. These, it was hoped, would effectively wreck any enemy aeroplane attempting a night time landing. The poles were transported by a trailer and tractor just on evening twilight, being collected at dawn next morning. One day the collection was late and a Hurricane made a landing, fortunately the pilot saw the poles in time and was able to avoid them. He had landed to enquire the way to Croydon aerodrome, and after the hasty collection of defence poles took off in a south-westerly direction. Another Hurricane landed with a damaged oil pipe after a dog fight. The pilot, wearing a flying helmet, parachute and somewhat casual clothes, which included grey flannel trousers, said he had just shot down two enemy air-craft. The damage was soon repaired and the aircraft returned to base.

153

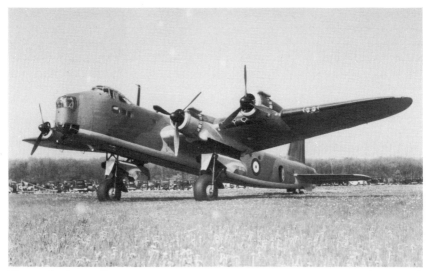

First production Stirling at Rochester (Short Bros)

In two raids, Rochester airfield was subjected to a considerable onslaught. Not all the bombs were on target. Nearby Davis Estate was also hit. (Kent Messenger)

Being a member of the Frindsbury Home Guard, John Chinery assisted the factory's Home Guard force in manning the earth slit trenches along the edge of the airfield, close to the factory complex. They were armed with rifles, whilst two of their number, using binoculars, acted as spotters. During air raid warnings the factory personnel would quickly make their way to several pre-determined deep shelters close to the factory. Warnings were frequent and, in one two-week period, only twelve hours of work was possible.

A prelude to the first of the Rochester airfield raids occurred on Sunday August 11th. On that day the inevitable air raid warning was given, followed by the appearance of one high flying enemy aeroplane. It was a twin engine affair, probably a Dornier, carrying out aerial reconnaissance duties. Cameras loaded, it was up-dating those earlier pre-war photographs. At the time, the eleventh production Stirling was parked on the concrete apron preparing for an engine test run. This particular Stirling was to receive a direct hit later in the week.

The first raid upon Rochester was originally planned for August 13th —'Eagle Day'. Heavily escorted German bombers, including Stukas, from Luflotte 2, failed on this occasion to find the airfield. Instead, they dropped their bombs, somewhat indiscriminantly, throughout the county of Kent. Some of these fell on Ramsgate, Ashford and Canterbury.

It was on August 15th that Rochester airfield received its first, and most serious, raid. John Chinery's task during an air raid was to record the fall of bombs. He was at his usual station, scanning the eastern skies. Through the haze, from the north-east, appeared a squadron of medium bomber aircraft flying in echelon formation.

Also there, on that day, was Cyril Gilks, now living in quiet retirement at Strood. He counted sixteen German Dornier bombers, rapidly losing height from around 10,000 feet. He remembers that some of the first people to see the raiders were a number of workers employed upon the construction of a new hangar for Stirling bombers. Somewhat vulnerable on the scaffolding erected above the hangar, they came down their ropes in something of a panic.

The raid itself took no longer than a couple of minutes, but during that time the area was saturated by countless incendiaries and high explosive bombs. Immediately after the raid Chinery left his trench and watched the Dorniers making a U-turn on their way back to base. On returning to the nearby factory buildings, following the 'all clear', he found a scene of widespread devastation. The main parts store was on fire, most of the hangar roofs were blown off whilst the number eleven Stirling had been completely torn apart. In all some five Stirlings were lost as a result of the raid, most of these being in the main assembly hangar.

There was also much general damage in the workshops with the office block, situated inside the assembly hangar, completely shattered. Fortunately, the massive square timber which temporarily supported a number of hangar trusses had not been blown down; if they had, then the massive roof would also have collapsed with many more Stirlings being damaged.

Rochester Airport 1980. Short Bros moving to Belfast in the 1950's cease to have an interest and the site is now owned by Marconi-Avionics. Civilian flying continues. (Len Pilkington)

Outside, a bomb had exploded on the concrete car park east of the hangar block. This had blown off the canteen roof and demolished a near side wall. To the amazement of vehicle owners they found that none of their cars had been damaged. A motor cycle, on the edge of the large bomb crater, still stood on its upright stand while a sports car, on the other side of the crater, only needed dusting down.

Despite the many hundreds of workers employed at Rochester during that air raid, there was only one fatality. A member of the fire service was sheltering inside the factory building and using one of the six foot high individual bell domes designed for fire watchers. Constructed of welded steel they were supposed to be bullet proof, and were generally considered very safe. On this occasion a bomb had exploded nearby and shrapnel had passed through the steel wall.

The second raid occurred on September 4th, when the airfield and factory again suffered a saturation raid. During this attack, to the consternation of all concerned, an incendiary penetrated the main factory and fell onto a pile of salvaged magnesium alloy fittings. These immediately ignited and were soon destroyed in a roaring mass of flames. The main paint store, to the east end of the hangar block, was also destroyed.

After the first raid, many of the personnel employed at Rochester suffered from 'jitters' every time an air raid warning was given. Instead of going to the allotted deep shelters sited near the factory, many ran across the airfield into the woods beyond so that they might be right out of the way of any bombs. These individuals now had a most frightening experience as a mass of incendiary bombs were off target and fell into these woods. Fortunately there was no loss of life.

Despite the limited loss of actual Stirlings during the first raid, considerable damage had, of course, been done to the factory area. A resumption of work was out of the question. The salvage of valuable machine tools was all that could be considered at this point. Thus, the few workers kept on at the airport factory (most were transferred elsewhere) found themselves removing piles of debris.

No further Stirlings were produced at Rochester that year. Instead, much of the salvaged machinery was re-located to other sites. The Short Brothers factory at Strood now became responsible for assembling some Stirlings during this period, as was the Great Western Railway factory at Swindon. Later, additional sub-contract work was carried out by Austins. The Rochester airport site was not, however, totally abandoned. In early 1941 the decision was taken to rebuild the factory and, from 1942 onwards, Stirlings were once again assembled there. It was an aeroplane which remained in production throughout the war, with the last Rochester built Stirling coming off the production line in 1945.

Fairey Battle 1 of 142 Squadron (K7696)   (P.J. Small)

Bomb damage to the huts in Eastchurch   (P.J. Small)

Chapter Ten

EASTCHURCH

By Philip MacDougall

Throughout 1940, due to faulty intelligence, the German High Command had the impression that Eastchurch was a Fighter Command station. It was for this singular reason that, on Tuesday August 13th, some thirty Dornier bombers converged on the airfield for the first of several daylight air raids.

For the Luftwaffe, this was no ordinary air raid. August the thirteenth was 'Eagle Day' — ADLER TAG — the day in which the Battle of Britain was to open in earnest. Already 'Eagle Day' had been cancelled once, having been set originally for August 10th, it had been put back due to unfavourable weather. Now, August 13th was set as the day in which the Luftwaffe would, over a short period of time, completely destroy the Royal Air Force. It was the day in which numerous devastating raids were to be carried out on a number of Kentish airfields, and certainly the day in which the Luftwaffe intended to show its true might.

ADLER TAG dawned cloudy and overcast. In France, visibility was very poor, whilst advance reconnaissance aircraft reported similar problems over south-east England. Yet 'Eagle Day' could not once again be cancelled . . . or could it? The German High Command was more than a little indecisive. But, at that very last moment, the order was given. ADLER TAG was to be delayed until the afternoon. The early morning bombing raids were to be aborted.

Not all those involved were informed of these changing plans. Already seventy-four Dornier Do.17's, of Kampfgeschwader 2, under the command of Oberst Johannes Fink, were airborne. Due to supply difficulties, radios in the leading aircraft were without the correct crystals. They were effectively cut off from all outside communication. Over Amiens they met up with their fighter escort, sixty Messerschmitt 110's of ZG/26. For their part, the Messerschmitts were more than aware of the new orders. Indeed, they even tried to inform the bombers. To do this, they adopted strange tactics of diving in front of the assembled bombers, in the hope that they would realize something was amiss. But all was to no avail.

Fink, seeing all this, merely concluded that the Messerschmitt pilots were suffering from natural over exuberance. Instead of turning back, he led the large force of bombers on to their pre-selected targets. The fighters, for their part, returned home.

The Dorniers were to be without any fighter escort, but the poor weather was to help conceal their position from the RAF. To start with, as they crossed the British coastline, spotters of the Royal Observer Corps, unable to see the bombers, wrongly charted their position. This now made it increasingly difficult for the several defence squadrons sent up to intercept. Only one of these units, 'Sailor'

159

Malan's 74 Squadron, made contact. This was over Whitstable, by which time the bombers were remarkably close to their target.

Over Sheppey, the bombers split in to two separate groups. One formation headed for the dockyard at Sheerness, whilst the other made for Eastchurch.

The airfield at Eastchurch, throughout 1940, was under the command of No. 16 Group Coastal Command. Like many of the other airfields in Kent, it had already played an important part in the war. Earlier, in May, it had hosted a fighter squadron flying cover over Dunkirk. Later the Blenheims of 35 and 53 Squadrons Coastal Command were posted to Eastchurch in order to carry out attacks upon the German invasion barges. From this point of view, then, Eastchurch was a reasonably important target, and as an airfield would have to be disposed of at some point. Yet it was not a Fighter Command airfield, and for the Germans this was the whole point of the raid.

As luck would have it, there was a total of five squadrons represented at Eastchurch on that Tuesday morning. The Blenheims of 35 Squadron were still stationed there whilst, that previous day, some new squadrons had flown into the airfield. All were caught on the ground by this German raid. Of these new squadrons, 12 and 142 were sister squadrons which operated Fairey Battles. Earlier they had been in France, giving support to the British Expeditionary Force. 12 Squadron — the 'dirty dozen' — had already proved its mettle with a number of attacks upon heavily defended targets, for which two members of the squadron had been awarded posthumous VCs. Both these squadrons were now at Eastchurch in the continuing campaign against the invasion barges mustering at Boulogne.

The other aircraft which had arrived that previous day were six Spitfires of 19 Squadron's 'B' flight together with the Spitfires of 266 Squadron. Even though they were both Fighter Command squadrons, their presence at Eastchurch was no more than coincidence. Yet, damage to Spitfires belonging to one of these squadrons did mean that the raid was not a total failure.

It was a few minutes after seven o'clock that bombs first began to land on the airfield. The thirty Dorniers of KG/2 had found their target. According to the records subsequently written up for 266 Squadron, they flew over in two waves, dropping over one hundred high explosive and incendiary bombs. All in all, the raid was fairly devastating. Considerable damage was done to the grass flying off area, but more serious was damage to the airfield buildings. All of the hangars received hits, with those used by 266 Squadron bursting into flames. Here one Spitfire was totally destroyed whilst three others were brought out before flames managed to reach them. Elsewhere on the airfield, 35 Squadron lost five Blenheims. Additionally, the operations block was destroyed and the airfield water supply together with the officers' mess damaged. All of 266 Squadron's ammunition was destroyed as was much equipment. Tragically, there were also a number of deaths — twelve in all — with over twenty-six serious injuries being recorded. The raid was well summed up by 12 Squadron's record book:

A Do.17, brought down, following a raid on Eastchurch during the summer of 1940.

"Eastchurch aerodrome and 'B' flight most thoroughly bombed."

The Dorniers, having done their worst, now headed for home. But by now the Royal Air Force was ready. A number of Hurricanes converged upon the unescorted bombers, and soon dispatched four of them. Fink would have lost considerably more of his command if it had not been for poor weather. A great number of the Dorniers took advantage of heavy cloud and did not re-appear until well over the Channel.

Back at Eastchurch, repairs were quickly undertaken. The numerous craters were soon repaired. Within ten hours the airfield was again usable. Nevertheless, the Luftwaffe claimed it as a totally destroyed Fighter Command airfield.

Aware that the bombers might return, it was considered imperative to move some of the squadrons away from Eastchurch. The result was that the two Spitfire units were ordered elsewhere. On August 14th 'B' flight of 12 Squadron returned to Fowlmere to rejoin the rest of 12 Squadron, whilst 266 was sent to Duxford.

During the following five weeks, Eastchurch was bombed on no less than eleven further occasions. Of these the worst was undoubtedly a raid on September 2nd in which four people were killed. It was just after mid-day when twelve enemy aircraft, in four separate waves, mounted a penetrating attack. 142 Squadron's record book states that a 'terrible explosion' occurred as the airfield's

161

main ammunition dump exploded. The NAAFI and airfield administration build-ings were destroyed as were the water mains and a number of hangars. Following this raid the airfield was abandoned until September 16th.

In many ways, though, the airfield at Eastchurch was able to return just a little of the medicine which it had been forced to take. The two Fairey Battle squadrons which were based there continued to mount a number of raids upon the invasion barges being assembled at Boulogne. Typical of these raids was one mounted by 142 Squadron on the afternoon of August 18th. On this occasion six Fairey Battles, loaded with 40-lb bombs, and flying at 5,000 feet, were able to report a number of fires started in the area of the port. One of their number, L5569, also reported a direct hit upon a seaplane. Anti-aircraft fire was intense throughout. Overall, though, their success was limited. The Battle was a near obsolete aeroplane, and hardly carried sufficient bomb load for its assigned task.

Twelve Squadron was also active later that day. Six of their aircraft attacked Boulogne, this time just as dusk was falling. Only four of the aircraft actually dropped their bombs as two others reported technical difficulties. No serious damage resulted from this raid, however. Both these squadrons remained at Eastchurch until September, frequently undertaking such duties.

Peter Small, who was part of 12 Squadron's ground staff, still vividly recalls those hectic five weeks in which Eastchurch seemed to be the main objective of virtually all Luftwaffe raids going. It was a time when, he recalls, the airfield was constantly pock marked with bomb craters. Another point he remembers is that the station had no anti-aircraft defences. There had been one 37mm gun, of World War One vintage, sited on a hill near the domestic quarters, but this had quickly become unserviceable after firing a few shots during one of the early raids. As the attacks became more frequent, they were often carried out at low level with fighters, usually 109's, and bombers strafing the airfield.

Small remembers a rumour, prevalent at the time, in which it was reckoned that Eastchurch was the secondary target for Chatham. It was stated that if there were any quantity of heavy vessels in harbour then they would be able to put up a barrage so heavy that the bombers altered course for Eastchurch. Some credit was given to this rumour by the fact that the airfield was frequently bombed by aircraft approaching from the west.

One peculiar incident occurred in mid-August. Again, the rumble of bombers was heard as they approached the airfield. Everyone, naturally enough, raced for cover. Then it was noticed that the black crosses were not evident on the aircraft wings — instead, roundels could be seen. Now everyone relaxed, and returned to their various jobs. That is until bombs started whistling down! The aircraft were French, captured during the fall of France and pressed into service. The insignias had remained unaltered. Those at Eastchurch thought it to be a bit of a dirty trick.

Eastchurch remained in the hands of Coastal Command until June 1941. It then ceased its attachment to this Command and became part of Technical Training Command on August 25th. As a result, the RAF Artillery School was

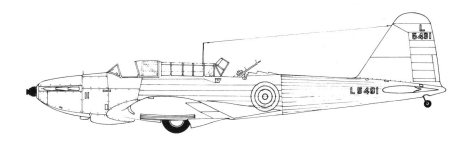

Fairey Battle Mk.1 12 Squadron Royal Air Force destroyed by enemy bombing, Eastchurch 12th August 1940

established at Eastchurch, together with a PAC installation. This did not mean that Eastchurch ceased a more active role in the war. During 1942 a number of 'lodger' squadrons were temporarily based here. Notably these included 65 and 165 Squadrons who were lodged there for the Dieppe raid. Using Spitfire Vb's, both squadrons undertook convoy protection duties during one of the most hectic days of the war.

A new phase in the service life of Eastchurch started on October 12th, 1942, when the airfield was attached to No. 72 Group Army Co-Operation Command, with the former Technical Command personnel remaining as a lodger unit. This new phase was in preparation for the future invasion of Europe. During the early summer of 1943 122 and 132 Squadrons flew army co-operation duties with the Canadian ground forces based in England.

The following year, with the invasion clearly in the offing, Eastchurch became predictably busier. In February the Hurri-bombers of 175 Squadron were heavily engaged upon attacking the newly discovered V1 sites, a role which was taken over in March by the Typhoons of 184 Squadron. On D-day itself, 266 Squadron occupied the airfield and was mounting attacks upon beach head targets. Once a beach head had been established Eastchurch, as a front line fighter station, was hosting the Typhoons of 183 and 263 Squadrons in their cab rank work.

It is at this point that the story of Eastchurch comes abruptly to an end. No permanent squadrons were attached to the station during the final year of the war and, instead, it concentrated upon its training duties. Once the war had ended the government could find no further use for the airfield and it was hastily abandoned by the RAF. The land was retained by the government, however, and became an open prison in 1949.

Chapter Eleven
LYMPNE AERODROME
By Roy S. Humphreys

It was late 1915 when Lympne village gave up one or two grass fields to the Royal Flying Corps who erected three canvas Bessonneau hangars near Otterpool Lane. The village is about seven miles from Folkestone and, like nearby Hawkinge, was ideally situated on top of the North Downs overlooking the English Channel. On a clear day both airfields were practically in sight of each other. Lympne castle, its magnificent medieval battlements standing proudly above the Romney Marshes, became the Officers quarters while the administration buildings and airmen's quarters were sited in an adjacent field.

Throughout 1916 various aircraft, destined for the RFC squadrons on the Western Front, used the rather sparse airfield facilities before leaving to join the Acceptance Parks on the Continent. In the following year the primitive hangars were being replaced by permanent Belfast Bow-strut types which were completed in 1918. With two hangars finished in June of that year and with a renewed offensive likely to take place on the Western Front, additional squadrons were required and 120 Squadron formed at the airfield with DH9 machines.

The unit was only just getting into its stride when the Armistice was signed. It looked very much as if it would be disbanded along with other squadrons. However, it was fortunate for them that they were selected to become the first RAF unit carrying air mail to Germany; flying to Maisoncelle in the first instance, but later extending their flights to Cologne. The success of this air mail service to the British Forces of Occupation was largely due to the squadron moving to Hawkinge where the bulk of the service was operated until its cessation later in 1919.

At the dawn of a new decade and when the Royal Air Force had been drastically reduced to just a few squadrons, the War Office, despite having spent thousands of pounds on its construction, decided to relinquish Lympne as a Military aerodrome. They did retain ownership however, and when commercial flights to the Continent began the aerodrome was provided by the Air Ministry with customs-clearance facilities, a wireless station, an illuminated beacon and floodlighting.

As early as March 1920 a civil cargo air service was operating from Leeds to Amsterdam, using Lympne for an intermediate stop. By 1922 a newspaper delivery flight to the Continent was in vogue landing at Paris, Ostend and Brussels.

With few restrictions or petty rules to worry about and relatively unsophisticated flying machines to operate, it is no wonder that civil aviation was able to develop rapidly. Lympne became the location for the three Light Aeroplane Trials of 1923, 1924 and 1926. Sponsored jointly by the Air Ministry and the Daily Mail, the competitions were held mainly to find suitable flying machines

Defiant Night Fighters practice low level flying at Lympne during August 1940
(Imperial War Museum)

for club use. Military adaptations, if designs proved suitable, would be an off-shoot. In any event, from 1926, the endurance trials and speed tests led eventually to the famous annual air races, in which participants competed for the Grosvenor Cup, Wakefield Cup and later the Folkestone Aero Trophy.

It was in 1928 that Lympne became the home of the Cinque Ports Flying Club, (CPFC), a club which fostered the internationally famous annual rallies when representatives from European flying clubs gathered in friendly rivalry. Probably because of its international flair, reputation and locality, Lympne was often chosen by civilian pilots as the place from which to start, or finish, their long distance record-breaking flights. There is an incredible list of famous pilots associated with Lympne, among them are C.W.A. Scott, Kingsford-Smith, Amy Johnson, Jean Batten, Tommy Rose and Jim Mollinson.

With the expansion of the RAF in the late 1930's, the Air Ministry decided to use Lympne more often and, during the summer months, a number of Auxiliary squadrons flew down for their annual training camps. The most notable of these Auxiliaries was, without doubt, 601 (County of London) Squadron, who I believe were usually known throughout the Royal Air Force, and most probably further afield, as the 'Millionaires Flying Club'. There are, as you can imagine, many stories associated with that unit whilst they enjoyed their summer camp routine, not least is the one which has been told and re-told over the years when members of the squadron, flying their own private aircraft, had bombed Hawkinge with toilet rolls and bags of flour!

At the height of the air expansion programme two light-bomber squadrons moved to Lympne on a permanent basis and, inevitably, the aerodrome came under Bomber Command. The Empire Air Days became a feature of modern recruitment techniques and many would-be pilots eagerly joined the Civil Air Guard for initial training after paying the £1 fee.

But the sounds and signs of war were drawing closer to England at that time. Incredibly, Lympne was transferred from Bomber to Training Command. No one quite knew why! Like Hawkinge, just a few miles away, and also now under Training Command, it seemed more obvious to use them both as fighter airfields. Perhaps it was to fool Hitler! It certainly fooled the locals when Lympne became H.M.S. Albatross! Naval recruits were suddenly walking the country lanes and byways in bell-bottomed trousers and white caps. The Naval Ensign looked out of place somehow, as it fluttered from the flag pole at the main gate.

Neville Chamberlain's rather sad voice spoke to the nation in September 1939, proclaiming war. Civilian flying almost ceased then. Most of the privately owned aircraft were sent to Sywell, Northamptonshire. Those remaining, for one reason or another, were locked in No. 2 hangar.

But despite the Navy's intrusion into Lympne's world of aviation, despite the thousands of sandbags, trenches and dugouts being hastily made, the civil airlines continued to make their commercial flights to and from the Continent, just able to keep ahead of Hitler's advancing Panzer Divisions.

Prior to, and during the evacuation of the British Expeditionary Forces at the beaches of Dunkirk, Lympne was actively engaged in administering to the Army Co-operation squadrons, quite apart from being the recipient of countless individual aircraft making good their escape. As for the Dunkirk period in particular, Lympne, in close co-operation with similar units at Hawkinge where No. 22 Group operated, dispatched the Lysander-equipped units to support the beleaguered British defenders of Calais by dropping supplies of food, water and ammunition.

By June 1940, Fighter Command had at last taken Lympne into its web of front-line airfields directly controlled by No. 11 Group, as a forward base and 'satellite' of the Biggin Hill Sector Station. The Navy had left for Newcastle-Under-Lyme. Now airmen were preparing for the air battles to come. It was in June and July that Goering's Luftwaffe concentrated their attacks upon Channel convoys, in much the same manner as they had done when dive-bombing troops and civilians retreating before them on the Continent. But how they managed to 'destroy' H.M.S. Albatross on July 3rd we may never know!

No one is sure why the aerodrome was singled out in that way, as Goering had not yet decided to launch his Adler Tag (Eagle Day) offensive, directed against the fighter airfields in the South East of England. Nevertheless, about ten bombers came over Lympne and dropped their bombs haphazardly around the area causing very little damage. No one fired back. It is, however, amusing to recall that Hitler's comic radio announcer, Lord Haw Haw, speaking from Germany that same evening, said that H.M.S. Albatross had been sunk in the Channel!

The first major air raid on Lympne occurred on August 12th, 1940, when the Dornier 17's of 1/KG2 flew in at little more than 800 feet at about 09.30 hrs. The three pairs of hangars received direct hits almost simultaneously with other buildings. The Station HQ blew up, together with offices, lounge, bar and the CPFC clubroom. In fact the only thing left unscathed was the Air Ministry Signal Station. Those neatly stored private aircraft in No. 2 hangar were all destroyed in the three-day blaze. Salvage work was hindered not only in delayed-action bombs scattered over a wide area, but by another air raid in the afternoon. To top it all, two Spitfires of 54 Squadron crash-landed on the field immediately afterwards.

Three days later the aerodrome was selected again. Over fifty Stuka dive-bombers, escorted by Messerschmitt fighters, swung into their characteristic streaming dive and rendered the airfield and camp non-operational for at least twenty days. One would have thought, after the previous successful raid on 12th, that there was nothing of value left to bomb. The Stuka pilots aimed their 500 kilo bombs at already shattered buildings. Direct hits were made on an already damaged sick quarters building. Water and electricity supply lines were cut in several places.

Airmen working non-stop since the earlier raid had been billeted in hastily evacuated private houses. Now, those very same houses had been blasted beyond immediate repair. One of the hazards was that no one knew for certain if the bombs, which had not gone off and could be clearly seen liberally scattered around, were actually delayed action types or had just refused to explode! Some airmen were observed going round these silent monsters on tip-toes!

Within about half an hour of the second raid the local Fire Service tender, from Hythe, roared through the main gate entrance with a crew hanging-on for grim death. In any other situation it might have been amusing, for their magnificent brass headwear, gleaming in the late evening sunlight, made them look like Roman Gladiators. They were professional firemen, but their professionalism was soon dampened by an RAF Warrant Officer who bellowed at them, "Get that b— thing out of here . . . there are unexploded bombs all over the b— place!". Without waiting to reply the driver reversed out into the main road.

Making another entrance through a hedge in Otterpool Lane, the fire crew came across an abandoned and burning RAF fire tender, its petrol tank still intact and likely to explode at any minute. Someone shouted "Stick a jet on it quickly!". As the cold water struck hot metal there was a sound exactly like machine-gun fire. Airmen in the immediate vicinity dived for cover. At least they knew what it was like to be under fire!

167

The whole experience had completely depressed the C.O. of the station, who appeared now and again at certain strategic positions to look at the absolute shambles around him. He could not believe his neat aerodrome, a prime example of pre-war civilian and military co-ordination, a famous name in aviation circles, was now burning — destroyed.

"Is there anything special you would like us to do?" enquired the Fire Chief. The C.O. took a long look at the hoses and rubble — water and flames, and replied, "What the hell's the use . . . do what you want . . . it's ruined!".

There was very little that could be done. The C.O. walked away and was soon lost amidst the smoke which curled and billowed into towering columns.

During the next two months the aerodrome, or to be more precise, what was left of it, was again attacked at least another half a dozen times by both bombers and fighter-bombers. Understandably, the airfield was out of action for very long periods, but what cannot be readily understood is why the Luftwaffe chiefs hammered it into the ground. Was it because of its international fame? It may have been just sheer bad luck that Lympne was almost totally destroyed. By all accounts Hawkinge should have been destroyed and not Lympne, because the former was more important to Fighter Command than the latter. But then Goering made many mistakes in attacking airfields in the South East of England which were not fighter orientated, such as Detling and Eastchurch.

Lympne never really recovered from its battering to be of any special use to Fighter Command during the Battle of Britain, other than being an emergency landing ground for aircraft in distress. It became a haven for damaged aircraft, mostly fighters, and many pilots were thankful that it still existed in that capacity. Squadron Leader Tom Gleave, C.O. of 72 Squadron, was more than happy to have Lympne beneath him on the occasion he was shot down within sight of it on September 1st. As for Sergeant Allard, of 58 Squadron, his Hurricane did a neat somersault in the centre of the field. There were many crashes of course, some pilots were more fortunate than others. Some of the young pilots walked away from their crashed aircraft with no more than a scratch or two. They were the lucky ones. It took more than an hour to cut one pilot from his bent and twisted cockpit. And then he died on the way to hospital.

Lympne received a number of spasmodic fighter-bomber attacks well into the spring of 1941, the Messerschmitts arriving most often from behind the aerodrome, that is to say from inland, enabling the pilots to strafe and drop their bombs, then drop out of sight down onto the Romney Marshes and out over the Channel. It was a favourite route, and a safe one, providing the raiders had sneaked in unnoticed. It must be said, in all fairness, that they were often undetected by either radar or Observer Corps posts until the last minute of their attack.

In the late spring of 1941, a specific use was found for Lympne when it became a second airfield for 91 Squadron, then based at Hawkinge. It was not often a fighter squadron could say it had two airfields from which to operate! But then 91 Squadron was not an ordinary fighter squadron. It was a specialised reconnaissance unit, which took full advantage of the basic facilities still existing at Lympne, by dispersing one flight of Spitfires during the summer months. The great advantage offered was that it enabled the squadron to keep their dawn and dusk patrols operational, as both airfields were subjected to low cloud base. Low cloud and sea mists often influenced operations at either one or other, but rarely both at the same time.

In the late summer of 1942 three squadrons of Spitfires arrived to take part in the Dieppe Landings and, like other aerodromes similarly engaged, the fighter station became 'closed' to other traffic.

In the spring of 1943 the comparatively new Hawker Typhoon aircraft, a low-level fighter and fighter-bomber which was eventually to make a name for itself in aviation history, arrived at Lympne with No. 1 Squadron. The unit felt their way cautiously through various evaluation tests which culminated in sweeps and intruder missions on particular enemy targets in Northern France later in the year. They were joined then by another Typhoon squadron, 609, whose own activities were considerably curtailed initially by certain engine modifications. The Sabre engine of the Typhoon was a most difficult power unit.

Lympne came into its own, as the saying goes, when the invasion of Europe required a formidable air strike back-up in the shape of 2nd Tactical Air Force. Over twenty squadrons were to operate from the aerodrome in just six months. As the Allied Offensive really got into its stride in Northern France, various squadrons of different nationalities, including Polish, Czech, Belgian, Canadian and Australian, used the Lympne facilities for either long or short periods. It was a busy period in the aerodrome's history. Bombs, rockets, cannon shells and light ammunition of nearly every known calibre were piled in dumps around the airfield perimeter. Spitfires, Hurricanes and Typhoons took off in ever increasing numbers to attack shipping, railways, enemy airfields, barracks and gun sites.

From the available statistics outlining Lympne's wartime contribution, there is no doubt in my mind that the 1944 period was the most important. By then, temporary buildings had been erected to accommodate both personnel and air-craft maintenance. Visiting squadrons, sometimes three at one time and operating as a Wing, dispersed their aircraft in such a way so that extra long-range fuel tanks and bomb or rocket racks could be fitted with the minimum of effort.

In between the Wing operations, individual aircraft were sent up to combat the V-1 menace, the pilotless missile with the one ton warhead, launched from their sites in the Pas de Calais area. The pilots became versatile in attacking Hitler's secret weapon sites with both bombs and rockets. The whole operation at Wing strength was usually neat, precise and under strict control. But their individualism when attacking a 'Doodlebug' (V-1), streaming across the Channel at nearly 400 mph, was like a shot in the arm. Typhoons and Spitfires, their pilots disregarding the formidable ack-ack barrage of rockets and shells, manoeuvred onto the missile's tail and usually opened fire at point-blank range. If the missile exploded the attacking fighter would usually end up going through the debris, quite unable to alter course. One method of stopping these robots was for a pilot to get one of his aircraft's wings under that of the missile, and then gently tip it off course. It worked like a charm.

There is the story of one pilot who had gone through one of these robot explosions. He came down in a field near Elham, watched by a Police Constable, who remembered the Typhoon levelling off above this field and just ploughing it up. Dust mingled with smoke and flames. P.C. Boot ran towards the wrecked aircraft but was amazed to find the pilot had disappeared from the cockpit. Then he noticed bits and pieces of burnt clothing on the ground. He followed the discarded clothing towards a small wood. There he saw the pilot standing in just underpants, shivering with shock. The first words spoken to P.C. Boot were, "Have you got a cigarette old man?"

In the spring of 1945, Flying Control ceased at Lympne and the resident 567 Squadron moved their Martinets and Hurricanes to Hawkings. In the last few months of the war the aerodrome had been used, once again, as an emergency landing ground, receiving a variety of aircraft from the Continent. It was during this period that Group Captain Rapheal, who had twice been C.O. of Manston airfield near Ramsgate, lost his life rather tragically, when his Spitfire collided with a huge Commando transport aircraft taxiing out on the field. Both passengers and crew of the Commando were also killed.

Inevitably, in the post-war period Lympne's activities returned to the civilian side of aviation and, naturally, the Cinque Ports Flying Club was the first to restart in April 1946. The first post-war air race, shades of the popular pre-war races, was held the following year with such diverse participants as a Firefly, Sea Fury, Spitfire, Vampire, Meteor and, believe it or not, a Walrus amphibian!

The CPFC experienced some difficulties in getting requisitioned buildings realeased from the Air Ministry for civilian use. For some quite unknown reason the Government department involved held a vice-like control.

But meanwhile the South Coast Flying Club had been formed, buildings or no buildings, and before long Wing Commander Hugh Kennard, who had started the new club, found his ranks swollen by CPFC members. In 1947 commercial flying recommenced with Air Cruise and Skyphotos, and in the following year Silver City Airways introduced their car-ferry service to the Continent. By 1950, the Skyways company came along with their DC3's, linking London and Paris with a popular coach-air service which extended into the 1960's, when the firm was re-named Skyways International; Dan Air took control of the successful coach-air service by which time the aerodrome had been re-named Ashford Airport.

But when the 1970's came along the passenger and freight services were transferred to Lydd airfield, now known as Ferryfield. Lympne was abandoned. It seemed incredible that, after all those years, Lympne, a name held in high esteem throughout the world, a name which says FLYING, was now to disappear. There are very few buildings left which hold any connection with the Royal Air Force. Those that do are just a few brick hutments which stand beside Otterpool Lane.

But it will be remembered.

Chapter Twelve
DEFENDING THE AIRFIELDS

By David G. Collyer

When it came to defending the airfields, the defences could be divided as follows:

Active — anti-aircraft guns, rockets and similar weapons, pillboxes and machine gun posts and to some extent searchlights. Also included under this heading would be the personnel, who would have had to defend the airfield if threatened by land attack.

Passive — measures taken to divert attacking aircraft, or to warn defences of their approach.

Radar, Observer Corps, balloons and searchlights, also the use of deceptions such as lights, false fires and even dummy airfields.

Anti-aircraft Weapons

Here are some examples of how anti-aircraft defences helped protect the Kent airfields during the attacks by the Luftwaffe in July—September 1940.

Mr Frank Cruttenden saw one of the raids on Hawkinge while taking shelter under a hedge near the aerodrome:

"On August 15th the airfield was bombed by Stukas. They lined up and dived, one after another, out of the sun with their engines shut off, so we heard no noise to warn us. There were about fifty of them, and they managed to hit one of the hangars, and some of the Administration buildings, but the runway was not touched. The A.A. gunners opened up and put them off."

The raid on Manston on 24th August was watched by young Douglas Brown of Ramsgate:

"When the bombers came in over the aerodrome, all hell broke loose. Anything that could fire had a go at them, and the formation broke up. They were so anxious to get out of the ack-ack fire that they threw away the majority of their bombs on Ramsgate, and quite a lot of people were killed. Some of the buildings on the airfield were hit and damaged, but the runway wasn't touched."

Mr Albert Stone, who was serving with the Royal Artillery A.A. guns on the Western Heights at Dover, recalls:

"They sent some of our 3.7 inch guns, the mobile ones, to Manston aerodrome when things were really bad there. They came back later after the worst of the raids had died down."

During World War One, anti-aircraft defences were a mixture of mostly unsuitable guns that other services could not use, but gradually a system of plotting and control was evolved. The best gun at that time was the 3 inch, which was still in use during World War Two. The Royal Naval Air Service used these guns to defend, amongst other sites, the Airship Station at Capel-le-Ferne near Folkestone. By the time the Gothas had started their raids on London in 1917, the Thanet gun defences were well organised and shot down two of these bombers during their last daylight raid on London on 22nd August.

Lack of money and manpower prevented the planned re-organisation of Ack-Ack defences during the 1920's and 1930's, and even as late as March 1940 there was a severe shortage of both. In 1938 London T.A. Infantry Units were being drafted into the Royal Artillery as gunners to try to remedy the situation.

The guns used to defend the Kent airfields during the Battle of Britain were the old 3 inch, with its high rate of fire, supplemented by the 40mm and 20mm Bofors guns, built under licence. Low level raiders were engaged by the obsolete Lewis machine gun, in either single, twin or sometimes quadruple mountings. At Manston, 600 Squadron developed their own anti-aircraft defences by using stripped-down Browning machine guns from their Blenheim night fighters. One gun was mounted on a pole and known as 'The Sheep Dipper', while another mounted on top of a round concrete tank was called 'The Armadillo'. Other guns were mounted on the crew room roof. Hispano machine-gun on home-made mountings, rifles from the armoury were used, and even lumps of chalk and earth were hurled at low-flying aircraft during the August raids, by frustrated airmen whose aircraft had been bombed.

Airfield Defences

As well as carrying out station routine duties, personnel were also involved with airfield defence. Squadron Leader W.L. 'Bill' Grout at Manston remembers this period vividly:

"Due to the reduced numbers of NCO's available for the various duties — Main Guard Commander — East Camp Commander — Orderly Sergeant — Coastal Defence Duty — Anti-Parachute Watch etc, these duties came round very frequently in addition to your own personal job. Thus, on the night of 23rd August, I was on Defence Duty with a squad of airmen, reinforced by Royal Engineers (who had dug the trenches) at Thorn Farm, Pegwell Bay. We were relieved at 0600 hrs on the 24th, and after returning to camp, had a clean-up, shave and breakfast and I then went to my office. Paper work was piling up, as I found that the other duties were taking their toll, and I was feeling almost worn out.

"Under the regulations existing at the start of the Battle of Britain, all personnel not engaged in other duties would parade outside the Station Headquarters at the issue of a 'Yellow Alert'. Some were equipped with rifles and

NCO's with revolvers (later replaced with Lewis guns) to help defend the airfield. We then waited until the 'Red Alert' was sounded, when those allocated for airfield defence would take up their posts, while the remainder made their way to the shelters.

"As a Senior NCO I was later issued with a Lewis gun which I kept by my desk all the time. Together with another NCO I would take up my position in a small sandbagged emplacement outside the Station H.Q. We blazed away at the enemy aircraft, but never expected to hit anything. However, it was very good for our morale to have something to do."

Pillboxes at Hawkinge airfield had machine guns mounted on their roofs, with brick or sandbag walls to protect the gunners from bullets and bomb splinters. At Detling there were hexagonal 'doughnut' shaped pillboxes with a raised section in the centre with a machine gun mounted on a post.

After the Battle of Britain there was no respite for the defences at the airfields. The 'hit and run' raids started, with low flying Bf.109 or FW.190 fighter-bombers sneaking across the Channel to drop their bombs, before high-tailing it back home. During the Battle of Britain the airfield defences were manned by Army personnel, but in 1942 the specially formed RAF Regiment took over. One of the first stations to see them was Manston. Here they achieved success when, on the 10th October 1942, a Focke Wulf 190 of 10/JG.26 was shot down by the RAF gunners.

To counter these raids, a squadron of Hawker Typhoons was based at Manston, but the similarity of silhouette to the FW.190 led to some tragic mistakes. In March 1943, Squadron Leader R. Beamont of 609 Squadron, at Manston, had to appeal to the local ack-ack gunners not to shoot down his squadron's Typhoons. On 1st June 1943 twelve FW.190's raided Margate and Broadstairs, and the Manston A.A. gunners brought down one of the raiders, but a Typhoon as well.

During the V-1 attacks from June to September 1944, anti-aircraft guns were re-deployed in mid-Kent, and then along the coast between Cookmere Haven, Sussex and St Margaret's Bay, near Dover. When the danger of conventional enemy attack had receded, many of the airfield A.A. defences were withdrawn to face the new menace.

Examples of airfield anti-aircraft units:—

West Malling — 264th A.A. Battery of 58th R.A. Regiment with two 3 inch guns.
Manston — Twin 3 inch gun batteries at Chalksole Farm, Cleve Court and Ozengall Grange — 308th A.A. Battery of 55th Regiment R.A.
Biggin Hill — 157th A.A. Battery of 55th Regiment R.A. with two twin 3 inch guns.
Hawkinge — Twin 3 inch gun batteries at Hope Farm and Arpinge Farm — 'A' Battery Royal Marines.

P.A.C. Rocket

Rockets

As early as 1935 the War Office had thought of the rocket as a cheap alternative to the anti-aircraft gun, and had started research at Woolwich Arsenal into 'un-rotated projectiles'. By late 1937 both 2 inch and 3 inch solid core, cordite powered rockets had been designed and built, the latter as an anti-aircraft weapon. But after secret trials numerous problems were discovered and the development delayed. At the start of the war the 2 inch rocket was converted into a weapon for the Navy as a counter to dive-bombers for use on ships. A land based version for airfield defence was so far advanced in May 1940 that the Prime Minister, Winston Churchill — a great supporter of innovation — ordered rocket batteries to be sited around ports and airfields to protect them from attack.

The official designation for the rockets was 'P.A.C.' which stood for Parachute and Cable. The rockets were like bullrushes, with a thickened head, thinner body, and were fired from a tube, the propellant being ignited by a small torch battery. When the bombers came over, the A.A. gunners selected to man the new weapons, were supposed to fire the rockets in salvos in front of them. When they reached about 2,000 feet two parachutes were deployed. The larger one carried the empty rocket, and a smaller one was at the end of a 1,000 feet length of thin cable, with a small mine at the end. The idea was that the cable would catch on the wing of the bomber and the parachute would drag it over until the mine touched the wing, exploded and blew the wing off.

Although the P.A.C. rocket batteries were installed at various airfields, amongst them being Manston and Biggin Hill, there is only one authenticated report of the device being successful in bringing down an enemy plane. At Biggin Hill, a Dornier was brought down during one of the heavy raids, and the name plate was salvaged from the bomber and afterwards presented to the rocket's inventor. However, with the numbers of aircraft which would have been over an airfield during the raid it was quite likely that the P.A.C. rockets would have hit something. It was fortunate that it was not a Hurricane or Spitfire.

Later in the war the Observer Corps posts along the coast were issued with rockets during the 'hit and run' raids. As the enemy fighter-bombers flew in at low level, the radar plotters had difficulty in spotting them quickly, and the raiders were often on their way back home before the defending fighters could be scrambled to intercept them. Therefore a system of standing patrols was started, and when enemy aircraft were sighted from one of the Observer Corps posts, a 'Totter' (code name) rocket was fired to bring the attention of the fighters to the position of the enemy.

During the V-1 attacks in 1944, a similar system was employed to pin point the flying bombs, a difficult target to spot — small, fast moving and camouflaged to merge with the terrain. These rockets burst with a cloud of white smoke and were known as 'Snowflakes'; other rockets producing a red cloud of smoke were used to warn fighters approaching the gun belt along the coast, or the balloon barrage on the outskirts of London.

Pillboxes and Ground Defences

Just as the coast of Kent, together with its military and naval installations, was protected by pillboxes, barbed wire entanglements, machine gun posts and trenches so were the airfields.

As early as January 1940 there were 'mobile pillboxes', which consisted of large concrete pipes on the backs of lorries and housing a Bren gun crew, and were designed to be driven onto the runways in the event of an attack by para-chutists or ground troops.

However, by the start of the Battle of Britain, all the Kent airfields had been equipped with more conventional strong points.

Type 24 'semi sunk' pillbox, Hawkinge

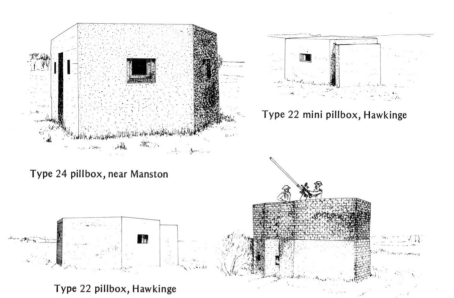

Type 24 pillbox, near Manston

Type 22 mini pillbox, Hawkinge

Type 22 pillbox, Hawkinge

Combined machine-gun/post, Hawkinge

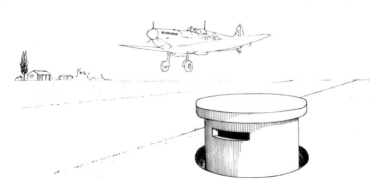

Pickett Hamilton pillbox shown in raised position

Original brick machine-gun pillbox, Detling. (Note original wide-splay loopholes for Bren guns and bricked up entrance. Built re Aug. 1940. (D.G. Collyer)

Mr Henry Wills, winner of the BBC Chronicle Award in 1979 for his research into pillboxes notes:

"These were built . . . with some designs specifically for the Air Ministry.

"An obscure drawing shows the hexagonal pattern as 'Type 22', the rectangular type with half roof and A.A. pillar as 'Type 23'. The 'Type 24' is hexagonal but one side longer than the others, and 'Type 25' is circular (Air Ministry pattern) . . . similar to Armco concrete pipes, and the square pattern is given as 'Type 26' . . . of course all could be modified by Army commands.

"In addition there were anti-aircraft positions which, in some cases, resembled pillboxes with a turret, although these may have been designed locally."

The most interesting type of airfield defence work was the 'Pickett Hamilton Retractable Fort', which consisted of two 10 feet diameter concrete pipes one within the other, the smaller one having a flat concrete roof and loop holes for rifles on Bren guns.

Several years ago some members of K.A.H.R.S. made a startling discovery at Hawkinge. For years the metal hatch covers had thought to have been drain manholes, as the tops of the retractable pillboxes, set flush with the earth, had been covered with grass. We stumbled across three of these sited alongside the main runway and dating back to Battle of Britain days. One of our party made the discovery when he lifted the hatch cover and daylight played on the compressed-air bottle and mechanism by which the forts would have been raised out of their pits, and lowered when not in use.

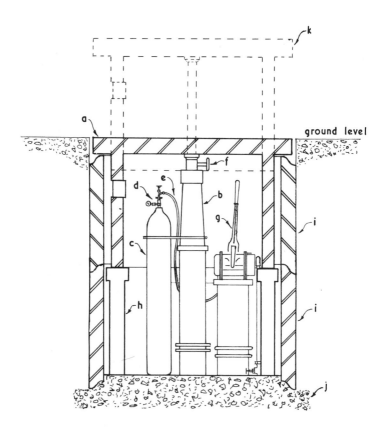

TYPICAL SECTION THROUGH PICKETT
HAMILTON RETRACTABLE PILLBOX.

Key

a Reinforced concrete turret (shown in retracted position).

b Pneumatic ram.

c Compressed air cylinder.

d Pressure gauge/valve assembly.

e Rubber tube to raising/lowering mechanism.

f Locking wheel to ram rod.

g Hand operated raising/lowering mechanism.

h Reinforced concrete turret supports, 8-off spaced in 4 groups of 2

i Spun concrete interlocking pipe sections.

j Concrete base.

k Turret, (raised position).

Mr Reg Curtis, of the Medway Military Research Group, provided the following information on an earlier design. There was an earlier version of the Retractable, this was the Pickett-Hamilton Counter-Balance Fort. This particular design was a ten foot diameter cylindrical concrete pit with a reinforced concrete vertically sliding head six-foot in diameter. The sliding head was connected to a counterweight by six wire ropes which passed over three pulleys. The pulleys were fixed to steel uprights. To operate the Fort a detachment of at least four men (it was designed to take six men with ample room for food and ammunition) entered through two steel trapdoors in the roof of the sliding head. Once inside, and when needed, all that had to be done was for the men to push up on the roof of the head and up popped the pillbox, and down came the counterweight to form a fire-step. Raising took four seconds while lowering took from ten to twelve seconds, with a minimum of four men. The cost of each Fort emplaced was between £230 and £250. It was recommended that at least three were required for each location.

Of the Forts discovered so far Hawkinge, West Malling and Detling are the later design worked by compressed air ram. One can imagine the difficulties the unfortunate soldiers would have had operating them. After having to negotiate the small hatchway in full kit, trying not to snag their webbing on the various projections inside, they would have been bent nearly double before raising operations began. By pumping vigorously on the handle to raise the top section, they would have had to poke their rifles or Bren gun out of the small firing slits. The whole process would have to have been repeated in reverse to allow friendly aircraft to land on the runway after the danger had passed.

Henry Wills provides some additional information on airfield defence. To control the defence of the airfield during a land attack, a special underground H.Q. was built with a communications centre and operations room, the whole thing being surmounted by an observation post with a 360° field of view. This was situated away from the main airfield buildings, and designs seem to vary from site to site.

With the threat of an invasion, when landings by parachutists or glider bourne troops were expected daily, all the station personnel were pressed into service to defend the aerodrome. At Hawkinge, on 6th September 1940, everybody down to cooks and clerks were issued with rifles and five rounds of ammunition, and told to make every shot tell as there was no more ammunition available. At Detling the pillboxes were later modified with additional concrete around the external walls, and all but two of the firing slits blanked off. Here the Army manned the pillboxes and many were killed in the big raid of 13th August 1940.

Camouflage

At the outbreak of hostilities there was a rush to camouflage all buildings at the airfields. At Manston this led to a somewhat strange situation, according to 'Bill' Grout:

"At the outbreak of the war, orders went out for all buildings to be camouflaged. As well as painting, the more important buildings were draped with netting to disguise their outlines. The W.D. Works Department (known to us as Works & Bricks) had just received a contract to redecorate the huts at Manston. One gang of painters arrived and carefully 'Snowcemed' the buildings in the camp, to be followed, almost immediately by another gang. These painters then proceeded to cover up their colleague's work with irregular patterns of black, fawn and green paint. When questioned about this, the foreman replied 'We have a contract to fulfill' — nobody had thought to cancel the original order for re-decoration!"

Should the Germans have captured Manston aerodrome intact, they would have been in for an unpleasant surprise. The 'Secret Army' of Home Guard Auxiliary Units who were detailed to stay behind in the event of invasion as guerilla fighters, made use of the old tunnels and caves left behind in the chalk from the smuggling days. One of the tunnels was found to lead from a chalkpit on the edge of the aerodrome right under the main runway. Although partially blocked along its length, it could have been used to enable the resistance fighters to gain access under cover of darkness. Explosive devices could have been planted on Luftwaffe aircraft and all sorts of confusion caused at the aerodrome. The process could have been repeated several times before the tunnel was discovered, but before it could be cleared for use, a bomb landed on the runway and blocked it completely.

Examples of Airfield Defences:

Pickett Hamilton Forts at Hawkinge, Detling and West Malling.
Type 22 pillboxes at Hawkinge, Manston.
Machine gun pillboxes, Detling.

Searchlights

Searchlights had been used in conjunction with anti-aircraft guns during World War One, and by February 1916 an outer ring of searchlights was positioned in the 'gun belt' around London. At the time it was stated: 'They are primarily intended to guide our aircraft defending the capital by signalling with the beam in the direction of the reported enemy raider'. But it is not difficult to imagine that the ack-ack gunners would have 'had-a-go' at any enemy aircraft or airship thus illuminated.

Like the 3.7 inch anti-aircraft guns, the searchlights were both static and mobile types, and the mobile units could be moved around the countryside according to how the raids on various airfields developed.

Mr Wally Kingsford was serving with the Royal Engineers searchlight unit during the thick of the daylight raids over Kent:

"By mid-September we were stationed at Molash, and I remember very well the 'Big Day' of raids on the 15th when the German bombers were coming over in droves. We felt very frustrated that it was daylight and that we couldn't do anything to help the fighters. Later on we were moved to Wheelbarrow Town, Stelling Minnis, then to Pratt's Farm, Woodnesborough — just by the church. Then we went on to the Royal St George's Golf Links and Princes Golf Links at Sandwich. The searchlights were mobile and could 'up sticks and away' at a moments notice . . . they were usually sited about twenty yards from the ack-ack guns."

At the start of the war the searchlights were placed on single sites, with a small detachment of ten men. They did not find much favour with the residents as the 'locals' thought that the searchlights would attract the attention of enemy bombers. This did happen on one occasion. Mr Frank Cruttenden recalls:

"If you go to the churchyard at Woodchurch you will see the graves of a searchlight crew who were killed when an enemy bomber flew down the searchlight beam and machine gunned the site."

The single light system did not work very well, and was replaced with clusters of triple lights regrouped onto larger sites, with anything up to sixty men. Most of these sites had no permanent accommodation for the crews who were still living under canvas during the winter of 1940 until huts could be built.

Eventually the fears of nearby residents were calmed and the searchlight crews welcomed into homes and public houses by local villagers.

There were also light machine guns (Lewis) positioned at the searchlight sites to protect them from attack by low flying aircraft, not without success.

Another task which the searchlight crews carried out was the less well known one of homing-in aircraft at night by laying the beam horizontally in the direction of the airfield runway. Not only friendly aircraft were homed-in, as on the night of 20th March 1943 when a Focke Wulf FW.190A-4 U8 of 2/SKG10 landed at Manston after being guided down by the local searchlight crew, the pilot having become lost whilst over Kent.

Where barrage balloons were sited in the vicinity of an airfield, as at Biggin Hill, the searchlight crews would illuminate the balloons if it was considered that a friendly aircraft was flying into their path.

During the V-1 attacks, the searchlights co-operated with the night fighters seeking their robot prey by marking the passage of the flying bombs, as well as giving warning of the proximity of the balloons. At the coast two searchlights were shown vertically as an aid to the night fighter pilots, their aircraft would be stacked around the beams to wait for their next victim launched from the sites in the Pas de Calais.

Examples of Searchlight Units:

Detling No. 1 Troop 313th Battery, 29th Regiment 56th A.A. Brigade.
Eastchurch No. 4 Troop 313th Battery, 29th Regiment 56th A.A. Brigade.

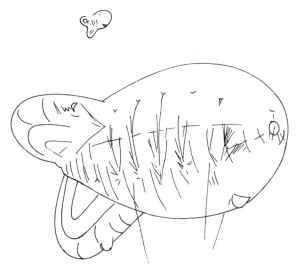

Barrage Balloon

Balloons

In September 1917, when the Gothas had started their night attacks on London, it was suggested that a 'balloon apron' be flown. This consisted of a line of balloons linked by wires, and vertical cables suspended between them. This would prevent any enemy bomber attacking at low level, and about twenty such 'aprons' were eventually sited in an arc from Tottenham, via Wanstead, Barking, Plumstead to Lewisham.

On one occasion the multi-engined 'Giant' Class aircraft R.12 flew into one of the balloon aprons and, although stopped in mid-air by the collision, it recovered after falling several thousands of feet. It was righted and managed to limp, badly damaged, to its lair near Ghent in Belgium.

The idea of a barrage balloon apron was revived in 1936 when it was proposed to ring London with them, but after due consideration it was decided that this would just force the enemy to fly higher, and a system of 'field sitings' was then developed. This entailed the sighting of the balloons at irregular intervals over a large area.

The main depot for the barrage balloons in the South East was at Kidbrook (now the site of a comprehensive school) which housed the Balloon Centre and Headquarters of No. 20 (County of London) RAF Company.

The Luftwaffe pilots took great delight in trying to shoot down the balloons, frequently attacking them with Bf.109 fighters, using their cannon shells to set fire to the 'gas bags'. Dover was especially subject to these attacks.

Balloons continued to fly over the ports and industrial areas throughout the following period of the war, and unfortunately it was not always enemy aircraft that fell victim to them. In November 1943, Flight Sergeant Spellin, a Canadian pilot with 609 Squadron from Manston, flew his Typhoon into a balloon cable, which he did not see as the balloon itself was airborne in low cloud.

As part of the defences against the V-1 attacks, the London barrage balloon belt was installed with a thick line of balloons flying at 45,000 feet. By 19th June 1944 there were 344 balloons covering Brasted, Westerham, Tatsfield and Ide Hill. Every conceivable space was used, even portions of railway embankment had a detachment camped thereon. The next day, the first V-1 was brought down by the Biggin Hill barrage, followed quickly by two more, but then a Mosquito was caught while chasing a V-1.

The Barrage Balloon Belt provided so much of a hazard to flying, that Biggin Hill and Gravesend, right in the midst of the forest of cables, were temporarily closed to aircraft during July and August 1944. When the V-1's ceased to arrive from France, after the capture of the launching sites on 5th September, Biggin Hill was reopened, but Gravesend remained non-operational, even after the balloons had been removed.

Examples of airfield Balloon Barrages

Manston — No. 1 Troop 'M' Balloon Company.

Radar

The establishment of Radar (or Radio Direction Finding) Stations in Kent began soon after the early experiments at Daventry and Bawdsey, with the planning of a chain of Early Warning stations around the south and east coasts.

One of the first stations to be planned was at Dunkirk, near Canterbury. This was in 1934, and by the next year experiments were carried out at Biggin Hill in order to investigate the possibility of intercepting enemy bombers in bad weather, and at night. Using Gloster Gladiators of 32 Squadron, and three Hawker Hinds to simulate the attacking bombers, the latter were flown in from France. One hundred per cent success was achieved in interception of the 'enemy'. During the Air Defence Exercises the following year, Fighter Command put up three squadrons of Bristol Bulldogs, four squadrons of Hawker Furies and a Gloster Gauntlet squadron in defence of Biggin Hill, all guided by radar.

By 1937 the radar stations at Dover and Dunkirk were handed over, and the four tall lattice masts, characteristic of the Chain Home stations dominated the skyline. At Dover, young Mr Harman was very interested in the structures appearing on the cliffs near Dover Castle:

"I was friendly with a carpenter who had been working at the Ferry Dock, and he suggested that I came up and took some snaps of his new job. I cycled

Swingate 1936. Radar Station (Recons. towers under construction) (J.G. Harman)

up to Swingate and took some pictures of the wooden masts he was constructing, I believe, with Columbian Pine. I took one looking up through the mast and entered it in a 'News Chronicle' unusual pictures competition. I did not get the prize, and perhaps it was just as well the picture was not published as Adolf might have had news of our secret weapon."

In November 1937 a Gloster Gauntlet of 32 Squadron was vectored onto a civilian airliner over the Thames Estuary, the first proper radar directed interception. At the time of Neville Chamberlain's flight to Munich in September 1938 all the coastal radar stations were on continuous watch, and they tracked the De Havilland Flamingo carrying the Prime Minister from Heston.

During the summer of 1939, radar stations tracked the Graf Zeppelin as it flew around the coast of England, and a few weeks later the whole radar chain was put on the alert. A flight of fifty aircraft was tracked, making straight across the North Sea to Britain. However, they turned back some seven miles from the Norfolk coast, and it was realised that we had been privy to the Luftwaffe's own Defence Exercises.

Swingate Radar Station 1936.
(Recons. towers under construction)
(J.G. Harman)

As well as the early warning Chain Home radar, there was Chain Home Low or C.H.L. radar stations which kept watch from the coast at Warden Bay, Whitstable, Foreness (near Margate), Fan Bay (near Dover) and The Warren, Folkestone. This radar had been developed from an Army request for a 'coast watching' radar for the Royal Artillery, and a Royal Navy request of a similar nature.

Instead of having tall steel or timber towers, the sites were very small, a brick built hut on top of which was a rotating aerial, driven by an airman who pedalled a wheel-less bicycle. The C.H.L. sets completed the chain along the coast-lines, and were completed just as war broke out, construction and installation of sets being undertaken rapidly during the first winter of the war.

A diary of events in 1940, given below, shows just what part the radar stations played in the defences of Kent, and its airfields, during the Battle of Britain. It also shows how they attracted the enemy's attention, and how their failure to function cost Kentish airfields dear.

July 19th — Dover radar plotted a big build up over Calais. 16.00 hrs Heavy raids coming in from France.
August 9th — Test Group 210 attack radar stations at Dover and Dunkirk with

185

250 kg bombs. At Dover buildings destroyed and towers sway, at Dunkirk a near miss by a 1,000 kg bomb moves the transmitter block several inches, two huts destroyed. Attackers Me.110 with bombs, escorted by Bf.109's, under Oblt. Otto Hintz (Dover) and Haupt. Walter Rubendorffer (Dunkirk).

August 12th — C.H.L. station at Eastchurch attacked. Eight Bf.109 fighter-bombers of Test Group 210 attack Dover radar, damage to towers and huts. After Swingate radar station had been bombed, the WAAF plotters were moved to Scotland.

August 15th — Enemy attacked Swingate C.H. and Foreness C.H.L. stations, latter station shut down when power cable cut. Service resumed by 1815 hrs when seventy aircraft were detected heading for Dover/Dungeness area. Rochester aerodrome attacked and badly damaged.

August 30th — Electrical failure puts S.E. coastal radar out of action. Detling bombed, disastrous raid on Biggin Hill.

August 31st — Dunkirk C.H.; and Foreness and Whitstable C.H.L. stations attacked and damaged.

September 13th — Between 0930 and 1130 hrs the coastal radar stations suffered some sort of jamming to signals.

September 15th — The Prime Minister visits No. 11 Group Headquarters, and watches plotters dealing with fierce air battles over Kent. Radar stations at Swingate, and three in Sussex, warned of build-up of enemy raids over Calais.

The Chain Home station at Dunkirk near Canterbury came under Manston for administrative purposes. This led to one amusing incident related by Squadron Leader 'Bill' Grout:

"At the end of 1939 a detachment of airmen arrived at Manston kitted out for overseas service. They had been informed that they were to be sent to 'Dunkirk' and assumed that they were to be part of the British Expeditionary Force in France. They were most disappointed to find that it was to Dunkirk near Canterbury, and not 'Dunkerque' in France."

Manston was responsible for supplying Dunkirk Radar Station with stores during the Battle of Britain, and one unsung heroine was Aircraftswoman Dean.

"She was known, inevitably, as 'Nellie'" (recalls Bill Grout) "and drove the Stores truck between Manston and Dunkirk throughout 1940. Despite bombs, shells or machine gun bullets, come Hell or High Water, the truck got through. If ever a woman deserved a medal, it was that woman."

A.C.2 Chris Vincent had a narrow escape during the bombing of Swingate on August 12th:

"Norman Blakemore, 'Jock' Maxwell, and I were attached to Swingate Radar Station, but did not work on the radar; we worked on radio (listening for German Kickenbien signals) in a hut on the second platform down one of

Fan Bay Battery — Radar Station (CHL Aerial Gantry)   (T.D. Crellin)

the masts. We climbed up the mast by means of a ladder with loops every few yards or so. After a few times we thought nothing of it, but I remember feeling a bit queasy at first.

"One day in August I was on duty when there was a sudden roar of engines — I rushed outside in time to be thrown off my feet, and to see three aircraft (as I thought) at my level, climbing away. I thought that they were Me.110's.

"One bomb fell at the base of the mast, taking away part of the platform opposite the one on which I was standing. I suppose that we were perhaps 300 feet up on the 361 foot mast."

After the Battle of Britain came the 'hit and run' raids, starting on Christmas Day 1941. Channel shipping, south coast towns, airfields and harbours were raided by bomb-carrying Bf.109's and FW.190's. The attacks were difficult to detect as the 'Jagbo's' (fighter-bombers) came in low over the sea, and with limited radar information, the ack-ack and air raid warning system often went into action after the attacks had been delivered.

To combat these sneak attacks, information from radar stations was delivered direct to the Sector Control, and anti-aircraft sites by land line, and additional radar stations were established to give early warning of the low-level attacks. At Richborough (Ash Road), near Sandwich, a Ground Combat Interceptor radar station was opened in July 1943, with its large rotating, rectangular aerial frame in a field some way from the main camp.

The V-1 attacks of 1944 provided a further challenge to the radar stations, and coverage was extended by the opening of the Microwave Early Warning radar at Pett Level, Sussex, and additional stations at Stonar, Sandwich and St Lawrence, near Ramsgate. Mobile units were also scattered along the coast to provide as complete a coverage as possible, as at Walmer Green, Deal where a mobile unit was placed near the lifeboat house.

Examples of radar stations in Kent:

Dover — Swingate C.H.; Fan Bay C.H.L.
Canterbury — Dunkirk C.H.
Folkestone — Little Switzerland C.H.L.
Whitstable — C.H.L.
Margate — Foreness C.H.L.
Warden Bay — C.H.L.
Deal — Hawksdown C.H.L.

The Observer Corps

As early as 1914 a system of 'Spotting' had been set up for reporting enemy aircraft or airships, the Police being requested to telephone the Admiralty if anything of a hostile nature was observed within sixty miles of London. The next year the system was extended to cover East Anglia, and the counties to the north and east of London, information being passed by the Admiralty to the War Office, who took over the system itself in 1916.

Areas particularly vulnerable to enemy attack were also covered, and a Coast Watching Corps was set up, using Coastguards, elderly military personnel and even Boy Scouts and Sea Cadets. The last two groups patrolled the cliffs and beaches on bicycles. The use of Police as observers was replaced by military observers at anti-aircraft and searchlight sites. When Major General Ashmore took over the re-organisation of the defence of London from the Gotha bomber raiders, a properly constituted Observer Corps was established.

All this was disbanded at the end of 1918, but in 1924 Major General Ashmore set up shop in the village Post Office at Cranbrook, to conduct a series of experiments using Special Constables to observe and plot a Sopwith Snipe of 32 Squadron flying a random course from Hawkinge, over nine posts in the Weald. Day and night tests proved successful and, after further trials the following year had proved that the system was feasible, more Observer Corps posts were established. The Headquarters of No. 1 Group was set up in Maidstone.

During the following years the Observer Corps plotted 'raids' during the annual Air Defence Exercises, and Coastguard Stations and Naval War Signal Stations were added to the chain of observation posts. All of this was carried out under a cloak of secrecy, the only notice that the Corps members had that an exercise was to be held locally was a small card which would appear in the window of the village Post Office with the words 'Forewarned is Forearmed'. This was later adopted by the Corps as their motto.

A patient build-up of the organisation bore fruit during the opening phases of

Martello Tower at Folkestone, as used by Royal Observer Corps for spotting. Another tower at Dymchurch was also used by the R.O.C.

the Battle of Britain, when the Luftwaffe started its attacks on convoys. Plots of raids were sent from the coastal posts, via the Group Headquarters, to the RAF sector controllers and No. 11 Group Headquarters, thus enabling fighters to be alerted.

The period from 24th August to 6th September 1940 brought the heaviest work load for the Observer Corps to deal with.

During the attack on Manston on 24th August, the main cable connecting it with Sector Control and No. 11 Group H.Q. was severed by bombs. The Controller at No. 1 Observer Group at Maidstone was asked by No. 11 Group H.Q. to try and ascertain just what the situation was at the airfield. Post A.1 at Minster was contacted, and Observer Ford hastily grabbed his bicycle and pedalled the mile or so to the aerodrome and returned with the necessary information.

On September 18th Post N.3 at Allhallows, on the edge of the Thames Estuary, put in a request to H.Q. for three delayed action (unexploded) bombs to be removed from near the post as 'it made the plotters uncomfortable' — a master piece of understatement.

Despite the attacks which left the airfields at Manston, Biggin Hill and Detling in a shambles, the Observer Corps continued to send their plots and the fighters were guided to the bomber streams with their help. In recognition of their contribution to the defence of the United Kingdom, King George VI granted the Corps the title 'Royal' on 11th April 1941, but their work was not finished.

During the 'hit and run' raids, Observer Corps plots were prefaced with the code word 'Rats' and messages of this type were sent, as a priority, straight to Sector Control who often had fighters on their way to the area before the complete plot was received. The Sector Controllers had Observer Corps maps to aid them identify the location of the plots, and in addition inland areas not already covered by the existing chain of posts were supplemented by Satellite Posts to help plot the raids.

Further modification of the system had to be made to deal with the V-1 attack, first reported by Observers E.E. Woodland and A.M. Wright on top of a Martello Tower at Dymchurch, sending the long awaited code word 'Diver'. Sector Controllers were now installed in the Maidstone Group H.Q. to ensure closer liaison between observers sending plots and the fighters patrolling ready to intercept the flying bombs. The Dartford Observer Corps post even managed to send reports of the vapour trails made by V-2 rockets from Holland on occasions.

As well as enemy aircraft, the Corps posts plotted friendly fighters; bombers on their night time excursions to bomb targets on the Continent; crippled aircraft were plotted until they reached an airfield or landing ground. In fact nearly everything which flew was plotted, and one entry in the logbook of the Littlestone post read "One carrier pigeon, flying west at 50 ft!".

Battle of Britain Observer Corps posts:

Allhallows, Ash next Sandwich, Barham, Bearsted, Bethersden, Borough Green, Brasted, Brookland, Canterbury, Chislet, Cliffe, Cranbrook, Dartford, Deal, Dover, Dungeness, Dymchurch, Eastchurch, Edenbridge, Eltham, Eythorne, Farningham, Folkestone, Hamstreet, Headcorn, Herne Bay, Hoo, Horsmonden, Kingsgate, Lenham, Linton, Lyminge, Minster in Thanet, Oare, Orpington, Pluckley, Rainham, Tonbridge, Sedlescombe, Sevington, Sheerness, Sheldwich Lees, Sittingbourne, Snodland, Tenterden, Wateringbury, Whitstable, and Wye.

Deception sites

The idea of using decoys to attract bombs away from genuine airfields had first been used before the Dunkirk evacuation. But only twin rows of flares in open country, one or two miles from the real airfield locations, had been used.

However, when these experimental sites started to attract bombs, the flares were replaced with a system of electric lights simulating a badly blacked-out airfield. Known as 'Q' sites, they duplicated emergency landing grounds by not only using landing lights, but taxi aprons, obstruction lights (red), landing 'V's,

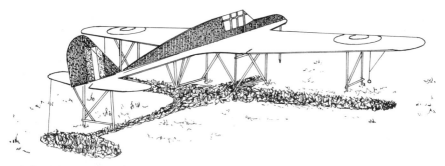

A flat dummy Hurricane assembled from a kit of parts. Appears three-dimensional when viewed from the air.

and even floodlights mounted on wires to simulate aircraft landing were used.

The 'Q' sites were introduced in June 1940, manned by two men to throw the switches at the opportune moment, also to light up the system of red lights to warn friendly aircraft not to land at the non-existent landing grounds.

Soon many Kent airfields had their phantom companions; Detling was matched by a site at Lenham; Manston by one at Ash Level on the nearby marshes; Hawkinge by one at Wooton, and a site on Cliffe Marshes was paired with Gravesend.

Should the enemy be tempted to bomb the 'Q' sites, they would expect to see the results of their actions, so in August 1940 the 'QF' site was invented. These consisted of numbers of metal baskets containing scrap timber, roofing felt and other inflammable material which was lit by electrically detonated incendiary bombs after the bomber stream had passed. By November there were some 30 'QF', or 'Starfish', sites in the country and Kent had some of its 'Q' sites modified. At other sites extra lights were supplied as at Lullingstone (for Biggin Hill) and at West Malling (where the 'Q' site at Collier Street was backed up by more lights at Hammer Dyke).

Having convinced the enemy that they had 'bombed' an airfield, evidence of the damage had to be produced for the occasional reconnaissance aircraft which ventured across the Channel. This was done by the supply of dummy bomb craters, painted on canvas sheets, which were laid on undamaged runways while the craters on the diversion sites were carefully repaired. The dummy craters were of two types, one for sunny days (with shadows) and one for dull days (without shadows). The former were turned periodically during the day as the sun changed its position.

The ultimate in deception was the true 'dummy airfield' for use by day, with runway, maintenance sheds, bomb dumps, etc. These were designed to simulate the small satellite airfields and were populated by 'aircraft' constructed by film set scenic designers, either of canvas and wood frames, or flat 'cardboard cut-out'

191

types. These sites, known as 'K' sites, had a complement of up to 30 men and were paired with the larger RAF stations. At Biggin Hill, the 'K' site was constructed on the site of the proposed civilian airport for London planned in the 1930's at Lullingstone. To add to the realism, two anti-aircraft guns were allocated to each 'K' site and genuine airfields were camouflaged by painting runways and buildings to blend with the surrounding countryside. Fake aircraft were also used at genuine airfields, and the enemy was not the only one to be deceived. One aircraftsman arriving at Manston found, what he at first thought, brand new Hurricanes stored in a hangar. He soon discovered, much to his mortification, that they were only dummies.

Squadron Leader Grout was responsible for pay as part of his duties at Manston. He recalls having to deliver pay to some airmen who were billetted at the village of Ash-next-Sandwich. It could well have been that these airmen were responsible for a 'K' site at Guilton, near the village, as a large field there had been used as an Emergency Landing Ground during World War 1. Another site, which has been shown on some maps as an airfield, is at Pembury near Tunbridge Wells. This could also have been another 'K' deception site.

Dummy airfields had been started in the phoney war in September 1939, and by early 1940 the first of them were operational, and by November there were sixty in use. However, they were more expensive — in time and manpower, to construct and did not have the same effect of drawing bombs as the 'Q' sites. By January 1942 most had been abandoned, although the 'K' site for Rochester airport at Gibralter Farm, Lidsing was retained to divert attention from the Short Brothers' factory at the airport.

This was not the end of the deceptions however, as during the elaborate scheme to convince the Germans that an invasion of France was contemplated in 1943, dummy aircraft and even gliders were positioned on airfields in Kent. Other instances of deceptions were a dummy 'flak tower' near the old World War 1 port at Richborough, and a fake radar station (with timber aerial towers and wood framed, canvas covered huts) near Manston built during the build-up to 'Operation Market Garden', the Arnhem landings.

So in their various ways the aforementioned methods of defence were to contribute to the survival of the Kentish airfields during the Battle of Britain. Even today relics of these can still be found — pillboxes and machine gun posts at Hawkinge, Detling and West Malling; the radar towers at Dunkirk and Dover and R.O.C. posts at Folkestone and Dover. With the present interest in preserving items of our recent history, is it not too much to hope that some of these items may be saved for the interest and education of future generations?